inspire

NANCY DOUGLAS

ANDREW BOON

NATIONAL GEOGRAPHIC LEARNING | CENGAGE Learning

Australia • Brazil • Japan • Korea • Mexico • Singapore • Spain • United Kingdom • United States

Inspire 1
Nancy Douglas and Andrew Boon

Publisher: Andrew Robinson

Executive Editor: Sean Bermingham

Senior Development Editor: Derek Mackrell

Editorial Assistant: Dylan Mitchell

Director of Global Marketing: Ian Martin

Product Marketing Manager: Lindsey Miller

Senior Content Project Manager: Tan Jin Hock

Manufacturing Planner: Mary Beth Hennebury

Compositor: Page 2, LLC.

Cover/Text Design: Creative Director: Christopher Roy, Art Director: Scott Baker, Designer: Alex Dull

Cover Photos: (front) Stephen Alvarez/ National Geographic Creative, (back) Henri Vandelanotte/Shutterstock.com

ISBN-13: 978-1-133-96357-8

ISBN-10: 1-133-96357-9

National Geographic Learning
20 Channel Center Street
Boston, MA 02210
USA

Cengage Learning is a leading provider of customized learning solutions with office locations around the globe, including Singapore, the United Kingdom, Australia, Mexico, Brazil, and Japan. Locate your local office at: **international.cengage.com/region**

Cengage Learning products are represented in Canada by Nelson Education, Ltd.

Visit National Geographic Learning online at **NGL.Cengage.com**

Visit our corporate website at **www.cengage.com**

Printed in the United States
1 2 3 4 5 6 7 — 18 17 16 15 14

Contents

Scope and Sequence

Unit	Topic	Lesson A: Listening	Conversation Focus
1	**Identity**	Faces of the World	Talking About Yourself / Hi, my name is Michael.
2	**Sports**	Do You Play Any Sports?	Talking About Sports / Do you play any sports?
Review 1	The Big Picture 1		
3	**The Night**	Nightlife	Talking About Evening Activities / I want to do something fun on Saturday night.
4	**Fashion**	Global Fashion	Talking About Clothes / I love your jacket.
Review 2	The Big Picture 2		
5	**Homes**	Four Similar Apartments	Talking About Homes / Where do you live?
6	**Buying & Selling**	Dubai Shopping Tour	Buying Something in a Shop / Excuse me. How much is this necklace?
Review 3	The Big Picture 3		
7	**Weather**	How's the Weather?	Talking About Weather / We have a holiday next month. Let's go somewhere.
8	**Mysteries**	Scary Monsters	Talking About Mysteries / Do you think Yetis are real?
Review 4	The Big Picture 4		
9	**Education**	The Power of Learning	Talking About Studying Abroad / I'm going to London this summer.
10	**Water**	Your Drinking Water	Talking About Water / How often do you drink bottled water?
Review 5	The Big Picture 5		

Unit Walkthrough

Unit Opener

Warm Up discussion questions introduce the unit topic.

Lesson A

Listening sections gradually progress from closed listening tasks to open discussion, providing the scaffolding students need.

Language models in speech bubbles provide examples.

Conversation sections provide both guided and personalized conversation practice.

Audio icons indicate CD and audio track numbers.

Listening activities practice a range of listening skills.

Lesson B

Reading passages are adapted and graded from authentic sources. They provide content input to act as a stimulus for discussion later in this section.

Reading comprehension questions check students' understanding of the reading passage.

A second **listening section** provides additional listening practice and further develops the ideas introduced in the reading passage.

Discussion sections introduce and practice functional language and expressions.

Split activities indicate in **red** where one student turns to the end of the book.

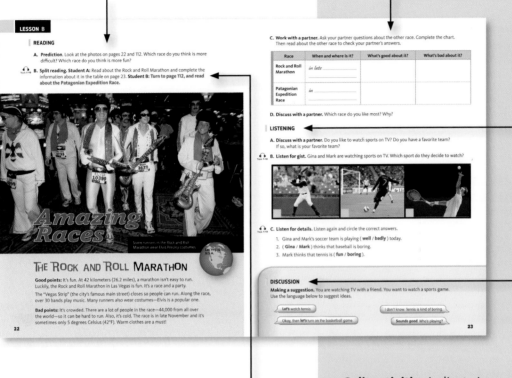

Video

Video activities give extra comprehension and vocabulary practice, and provide opportunities for authentic input, acting as a springboard for discussion.

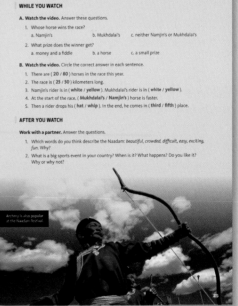

Unit Walkthrough

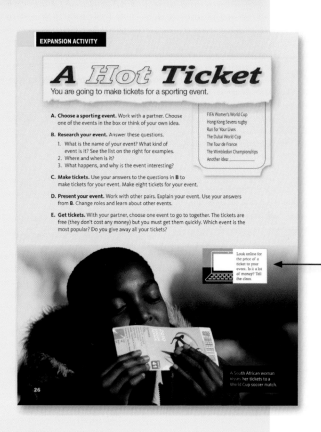

Expansion Activity

Expansion activities encourage students to use the language they've encountered in the unit and extend themselves in freer practice.

Tip boxes provide suggestions for ways students can use technology, such as cell phones to assist them.

Unit Notes

Project ideas usually build upon the Expansion Activity, and provide suggestions for ways in which students can take their learning beyond the classroom.

Unit notes at the back of the book provide additional material for split activities, as well as language notes, and suggestions for additional activities.

Target vocabulary provides definitions for key topic related vocabulary from the unit.

Important language gives a summary of language structures from the unit.

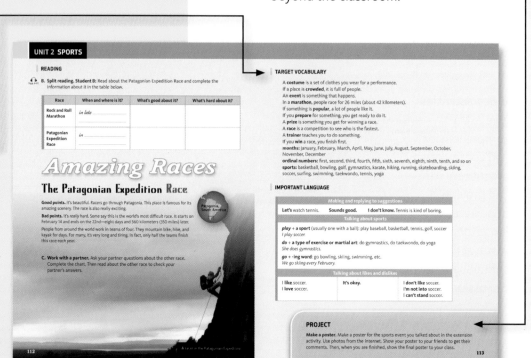

The Big Picture

There are five Big Picture sections, one after every two units. These sections review the previous two units and allow further opportunities for discussion.

Observation and discussion activities use the large photo to encourage communication and language practice.

Caption competition encourages students to think creatively about the image.

A stunning photo acts as a motivating prompt for discussion.

Review activities recycle and practice key language and vocabulary from the previous two units.

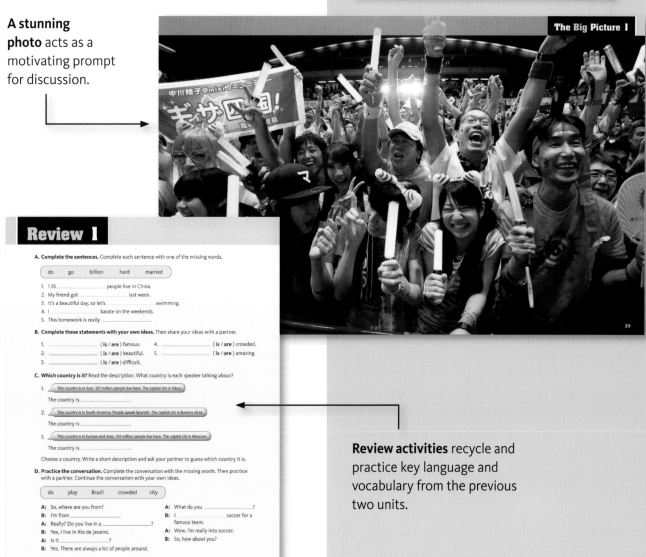

Acknowledgments

I would like to thank everyone who participated in the development of this series. Special thanks go to publisher Andrew Robinson for inviting me to be a part of this project, to Derek Mackrell for his editorial expertise and encouragement, and to Andy Boon for his invaluable support and inspiration. I am also grateful to my husband Jorge and daughter Jasmine for the love and encouragement they provided during the writing of this book.

Nancy Douglas

I would like to thank my wonderful co-author and editorial team for their enthusiasm, ideas, and work throughout the Inspire project. I would also like to thank all the students I have ever taught—you guys ARE the inspiration!

Andrew Boon

The Authors and Publishers would like to thank the following teaching professionals for their valuable feedback during the development of this series.

Jennifer Alicea, UPR Ponce, Puerto Rico, United States; **Grace Bishop**, Houston Community College, Houston, United States; **Leonardo Escobar**, Universidad Manuela Beltra, Bogotá, Colombia; **David Fairweather**, Asahikawa Medical University, Hokkaido, Japan; **Wendy M. Gough**, St. Mary College/Nunoike Gaigo Senmon Gakko, Nagoya, Japan; **Erica Harris**, Lewis & Clark College, Portland, United States; **Ikuko Kashiwabara**, Osaka Electro-Communication University, Neyagawa, Japan; **Maureen Kelbert**, Vancouver Community College, Vancouver, Canada; **Jungryul Kim**, Korea National University of Education, Cheongwon, South Korea; **Bridget McDonald**, ELC Boston, Boston, United States; **Jill McDonough**, South Seattle Community College, Seattle, United States; **Kent McLeod**, UT Arlington English Language Institute, Mansfield, United States; **Donna Moore**, Hawaii Community College, Hilo, United States; **Nancy Nystrom**, University of Texas at San Antonio, San Antonio, United States; **Jane O'Connor**, Emory College of Arts and Sciences, Decatur, United States; **Elizabeth Ortiz**, COPEI-COPOL English Institute, Guayaquil, Ecuador; **Maeran Park**, Bukyoung National University, Busan, South Korea; **Terri Rapoport**, ELS Educational Services, Inc., Princeton, United States; **Amy Renehan**, University of Washington, Seattle, United States; **Greg Rouault**, Konan University, Hirao School of Management, Nishinomiya, Japan; **Elena Sapp**, INTO Oregon State University, Corvallis, United States; **Anne-Marie Schlender**, Austin Community College, Austin, United States; **Karen Shock**, Savannah College of Art and Design, Atlanta, United States; **Julie Thornton**, CSULB American Language Institute, Santa Ana, United States; **Rosa E. Vasquez Fernandez**, John F. Kennedy Institute of Languages, Inc., STI, Dominican Republic; **Matthew Walters**, Hongik University, Seoul, South Korea; **Christie Ward**, Central Connecticut State University, New Britain, United States; **Matthew Watterson**, Hongik University, Mapo-Gu, South Korea; **Chris Willson**, Meio University, Okinawa, Japan; **Kyungsook Yeum**, Sookmyoung Women's University, Seoul, South Korea

Identity

This photo is made by joining 190,000 different photos.

Faces of the World

1 Country _____ First name **A** *Eva* _____ First name **B** *A* _____

2 Country _____ First name *M* _____

3 Country _____ First name *M* _____

4 Country _____ First name *S* _____

5 Country _____ First name *H* _____

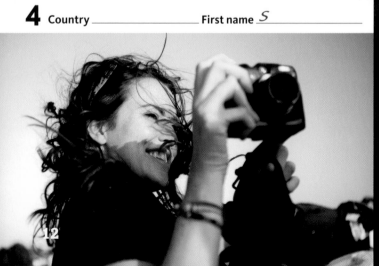

LISTENING

A. Match countries. Match the countries in the box (**a** to **h**) with the flags on the map. Then listen and check.

> **a.** Argentina **b.** Brazil **c.** China **d.** Iran **e.** Japan **f.** Malaysia **g.** the U.K. **h.** the U.S.

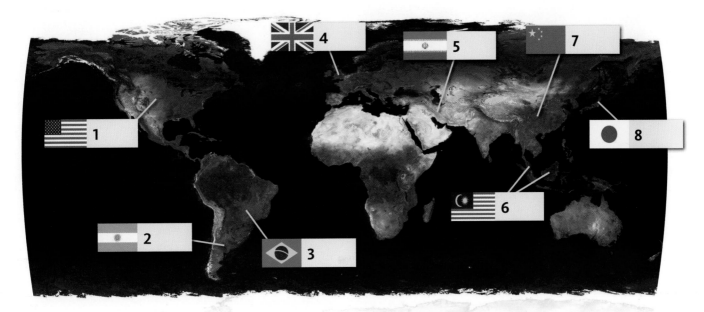

B. Listen for countries. Where is each person on page 12 from? Guess. Then listen and write the country on each photo.

C. Listen for spelling. Write each person's name.

D. Talk with a partner. Point to a photo. Tell a partner about the person or people.

> His name is . . . He's from . . .

CONVERSATION

A. Listen to the conversation.

> A: Hi, my name is <u>Michael</u>.
>
> B: Hi, <u>Michael</u>. I'm <u>Sofia</u>.
>
> A: Great to meet you, <u>Sofia</u>.
>
> B: It's nice to meet you, too. Where are you from?
>
> A: I'm from <u>the U.K.</u> And you?
>
> B: <u>Brazil</u>. / <u>Me too</u>.

B. Practice with a partner. Use your own name and country.

C. Practice again. Talk to three new partners.

13

ARE YOU TYPICAL?

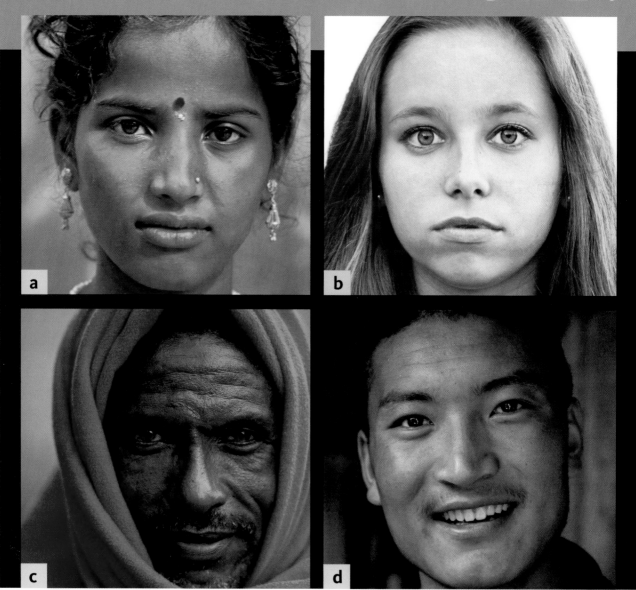

Today, there are over seven billion (7,000,000,000) people on Earth in _____
countries. We speak over _____ languages. We are different, but in some
ways we are similar, too. In a world of billions of people, there is a typical person.

• The typical person on Earth is male. (There are more men than women.)

• He is _____ years old and is _____ centimeters
(about _____ feet _____ inches) tall.

• The most typical person lives in a city and has a cell phone.

• He also speaks Mandarin Chinese. (It's the most spoken language in the world, with more
than _____ million speakers.)

Today, there are over _____ million "typical people" on Earth. Are you similar to them in
any way? The answer is probably "yes."

READING

A. Skim. Who is the world's most typical person? Read the passage quickly and (circle) the photo (**a–d**).

B. Listen for numbers. Listen and write the numbers from the box in the reading passage. One is extra.

5	8	9	28	75	174	195	900	7,000

C. Think about it. Work with a partner. Are you similar to or different from the person in the photo? Explain with sentences **1–6** below.

1. I'm a (**man / woman**).

2. I'm _____ years old.

3. I'm _____ centimeters tall.

4. I (**live / don't live**) in a city.

5. I (**speak / don't speak**) Chinese.

6. I (**have / don't have**) a cell phone.

> I'm different. I'm a woman. Also, I'm nineteen.

LISTENING

A. Listen for questions. A census worker is asking a woman questions. Number the questions **1** to **5** in the order he asks them.

Census Form

- [ ] What's your name? _____
- [ ] How old are you? _____
- [ ] Are you married or single? _____
- [ ] Where are you from? _____
- [ ] What do you do? _____

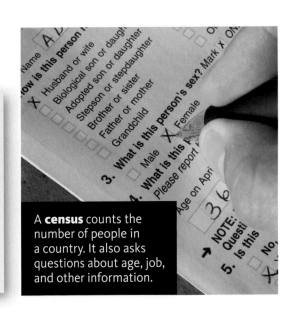

A **census** counts the number of people in a country. It also asks questions about age, job, and other information.

B. Listen for details. Write the woman's answers. Use one or two words or numbers.

DISCUSSION

Asking for personal information. Work with a partner. Ask and answer the census questions above. Think of two extra questions and ask your partner.

> How many people are there in your family?

> There are five: my mother, my father, my two brothers, and me.

The Global Village

New York City, U.S.A.

Queens is a very diverse area. People from many different countries live there.

BEFORE YOU WATCH

About the video. Queens is an area in New York City. It has over two million people. Many of these people are **immigrants** from other countries. Each group has its own language and **culture**. For this reason, Queens is very **diverse**.

A. Vocabulary matching. Read **About the video**. Complete these sentences using the words in **blue**.

1. There are students from Asia, Europe, and South America in this class. It is very

   _____.

2. When you live in another country, you learn about its _____.

3. There are a lot of Chinese _____ in Brazil. Most live and work in Sao Paulo.

B. Work with a partner. Answer the questions.

1. Where is Queens?

2. Why is Queens special?

WHILE YOU WATCH

A. Watch the video. Complete the sentences. Circle the correct number or word.

1. (**15 / 50**) percent of the people in Queens are from another country.

2. These people come from (**100 / 200**) different nations.

3. They speak almost (**50 / 150**) different languages.

4. For now, Queens is the most diverse place in the (**U.S. / world**).

B. Watch again. Look at the photos below. Circle the answers in each sentence below.

A She's (**Indian** / **Turkish**).

B Her mom is (**Korean** / **Japanese**). Her father is (**German, Irish, and English** / **Mexican, Russian, and Iranian**).

C Her grandparents and great-grandparents are (**Native American** / **Puerto Rican**).

AFTER YOU WATCH

A. Complete the sentences with your ideas. Then answer the questions.

1. In my city, there are (**some** / **a lot of**) immigrants.

   • Where are they from?

   • What language(s) do they speak?

   • Where do they live—which area(s)?

2. I know someone from another country. (**His** / **Her**) name is _____.

   (**He** / **She**) is from _____.

> I know someone from Brazil. His name is Tomas. We're friends on Facebook.

B. Work in a small group. Talk about your answers in **A** together.

People in Queens at the Indian festival of Holi

17

A Class Survey

Who is a typical student in your class? Do a survey and find out.

A. What are you like? Complete questions **1** to **5** using the words in the box. Then write your answers to the questions in the table.

> are   do   have   married   old

1. How _____ are you?
2. Where _____ you from?
3. Are you _____, single, or seeing someone?

4. Do you _____ a job? (If yes, what is it?)
5. _____ you have a cell phone? (If yes, what kind?)

	1. Age?	2. Hometown?	3. Relationship?	4. Job?	5. Phone?
You					
Partner 1					
Partner 2					
Partner 3					
Partner 4					

B. Work in a group of five people. Take turns. Tell everyone in the group your answers. Together, make one chart with everyone's answers.

C. Share your results. Put your chart on the board.

D. Make a poster. With your group, read all the charts on the board. Make a poster about a typical person in your class.

E. Show your poster to another group. Tell them about it. Are your posters the same?

> Look online to find census information about your country. What is a typical person in your country like?

Students in a language class in Peru

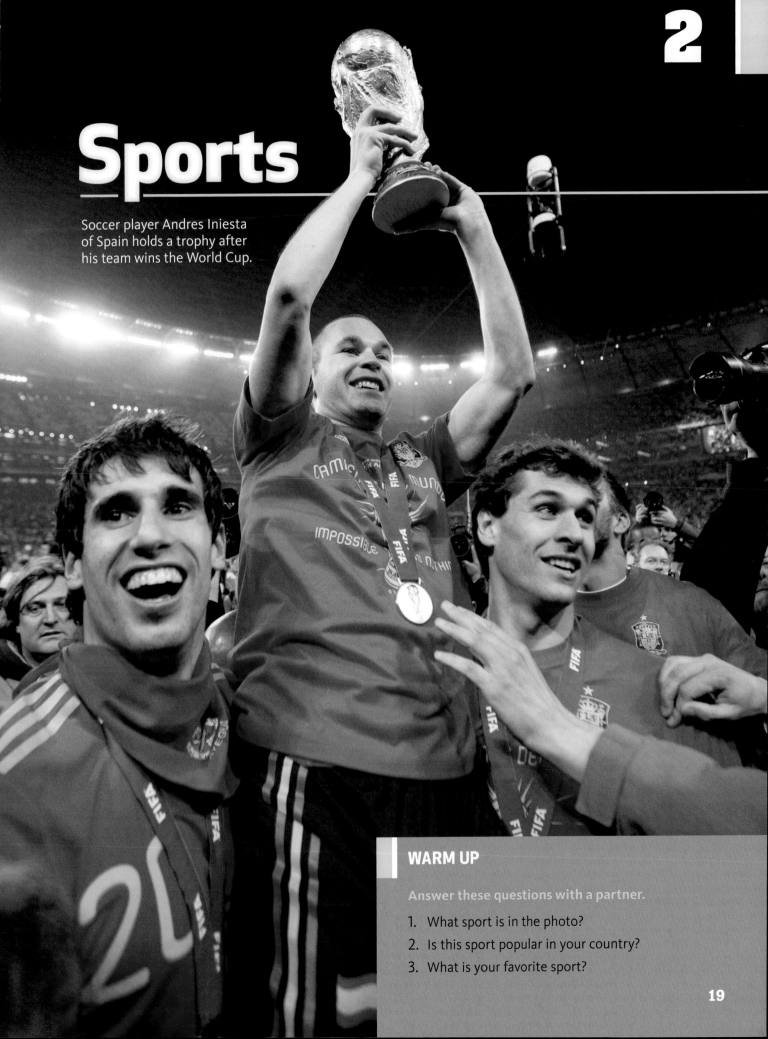

Sports

Soccer player Andres Iniesta of Spain holds a trophy after his team wins the World Cup.

WARM UP

Answer these questions with a partner.

1. What sport is in the photo?
2. Is this sport popular in your country?
3. What is your favorite sport?

DO YOU PLAY ANY SPORTS?

Baseball fans watch a game in Montreal, Canada.

LISTENING

Track 1-06

A. Identifying sports verbs. Look at the sports and activities in the box below. Which use the verb *play*, which use the verb *do*, and which use the verb *go*? Write them in the table. Then listen and check your answers.

| basketball | bowling | golf | running | skateboarding | skiing |
| soccer | surfing | swimming | taekwondo | tennis | yoga |

You *play* . . .	You *do* . . .	You *go* . . .
baseball	*gymnastics*	*cycling*

B. Listen for details. What sports do people in each country like to watch? Write them in the table.

Speaker	From	Popular sports people watch	Speaker's favorite(s)
Hiro	Japan	baseball, soccer, and _____	
Isabel	Mexico	soccer, _____, and basketball	
Ryan	Australia	rugby, cricket, and _____	

 C. Listen for opinions. What is each speaker's favorite sport? Write the sport in the table. Speakers may have two favorite sports.

D. Discuss with a partner. Which sports or activities are popular among your friends?

> A lot of people in my area go surfing, especially in summer.

CONVERSATION

 A. Listen to the conversation.

A: Do you play any sports?

B: Yeah, I play <u>tennis</u>. I also do <u>gymnastics</u>. How about you?

                                                                soccer / taekwondo
golf / karate
hockey / yoga

A: No, not really. Sometimes, I go <u>bowling</u> with my friends.

                                                         surfing
hiking
skiing
rollerblading

B: Do you like <u>soccer</u>?

                                                    tennis

A: Yeah, it's OK. I don't play it, but sometimes I watch it on TV.   basketball
                                                     baseball

B: Me too.

B. Practice with a partner. Use the words on the right.

C. Practice again. Talk about sports you like.

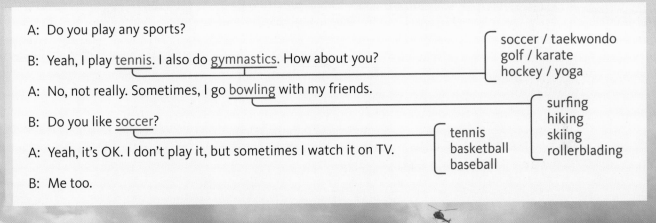

Cyclists race in the Tour de France.

READING

A. **Prediction**. Look at the photos on pages 22 and 112. Which race do you think is more difficult? Which race do you think is more fun?

Track 1-10

B. **Split reading. Student A:** Read about the Rock and Roll Marathon and complete the information about it in the table on page 23. **Student B: Turn to page 112, and read about the Patagonian Expedition Race.**

Amazing Races

Some runners in the Rock and Roll Marathon wear Elvis Presley costumes.

Las Vegas, U.S.A.

The Rock and Roll Marathon

Good points: It's fun. At 42 kilometers (26.2 miles), a marathon isn't easy to run. Luckily, the Rock and Roll Marathon in Las Vegas is fun. It's a race and a party.

The "Vegas Strip" (the city's famous main street) closes so people can run. Along the race, over 30 bands play music. Many runners also wear costumes—Elvis is a popular one.

Bad points: It's crowded. There are a lot of people in the race—44,000 from all over the world—so it can be hard to run. Also, it's cold. The race is in late November and it's sometimes only 5 degrees Celsius (42°F). Warm clothes are a must!

C. Work with a partner. Ask your partner questions about the other race. Complete the chart. Then read about the other race to check your partner's answers.

Race	When and where is it?	What's good about it?	What's bad about it?
Rock and Roll Marathon	*in late* _____ _____		
Patagonian Expedition Race	*in* _____ _____		

D. Discuss with a partner. Which race do you like most? Why?

LISTENING

A. Discuss with a partner. Do you like to watch sports on TV? Do you have a favorite team? If so, what is your favorite team?

Track 1-12

B. Listen for gist. Gina and Mark are watching sports on TV. Which sport do they decide to watch?

C. Listen for details. Listen again and circle the correct answers.
Track 1-12

1. Gina and Mark's soccer team is playing (**well** / **badly**) today.

2. (**Gina** / **Mark**) thinks that baseball is boring.

3. Mark thinks that tennis is (**fun** / **boring**).

DISCUSSION

Making a suggestion. You are watching TV with a friend. You want to watch a sports game. Use the language below to suggest ideas.

> **Let's** watch tennis.

> I don't know. Tennis is kind of boring.

> Okay, then **let's** turn on the basketball game.

> **Sounds good.** Who's playing?

23

Mongolian Horse Race

whip

Mongolia

Riders race horses at the Naadam festival in Mongolia.

BEFORE YOU WATCH

About the video. The Naadam is a Mongolian sports festival. It happens every year from July 11–13, outside Ulaanbaatar, the capital city of Mongolia. There are many sports events at the Naadam. The most popular event is the horse race.

Vocabulary matching. Read the definitions below. Then complete the information below using the words in **blue**.

a. If you **prepare** for something, you get ready to do it.

b. A **prize** is something you get for winning a race.

c. **Trainers** teach you to do something.

d. If you **win** a race, you finish first.

In the video, you will meet two men: Namjin and Mukhdalai. Namjin and Mukhdalai are
_____ . The two men teach boys to ride horses in the Naadam. These
boys _____ for the race for many months. Each man wants his horse to
_____ the race. The first five horses to finish the race get
a _____ .

WHILE YOU WATCH

A. Watch the video. Answer these questions.

1. Whose horse wins the race?

   a. Namjin's b. Mukhdalai's c. Neither Namjin's nor Mukhdalai's

2. What prize does the winner get?

   a. money and a fiddle b. a horse c. a small prize

B. Watch again. Circle the correct answer in each sentence.

1. There are (**20 / 80**) horses in the race this year.
2. The race is (**25 / 50**) kilometers long.
3. Namjin's rider is in (**white / yellow**). Mukhdalai's rider is in (**white / yellow**).
4. At the start of the race, (**Mukhdalai's / Namjin's**) horse is faster.
5. Then a rider drops his (**hat / whip**). In the end, he comes in (**third / fifth**) place.

AFTER YOU WATCH

Work with a partner. Answer the questions.

1. Which words do you think describe the Naadam: *beautiful, crowded, difficult, easy, exciting, fun*. Why?
2. What is a big sports event in your country? When is it? What happens? Do you like it? Why or why not?

Archery is also popular at the Naadam festival.

A Hot Ticket

You are going to make tickets for a sporting event.

A. Choose a sporting event. Work with a partner. Choose one of the events in the box or think of your own idea.

B. Research your event. Answer these questions.

1. What is the name of your event? What kind of event is it? See the list on the right for examples.
2. Where and when is it?
3. What happens, and why is the event interesting?

FIFA Women's World Cup

Hong Kong Sevens rugby

Run for Your Lives

The Dubai World Cup

The Tour de France

The Wimbledon Championships

Another idea: _____

C. Make tickets. Use your answers to the questions in **B** to make tickets for your event. Make eight tickets for your event.

D. Present your event. Work with other pairs. Explain your event. Use your answers from **B**. Change roles and learn about other events.

E. Get tickets. With your partner, choose one event to go to together. The tickets are free (they don't cost any money) but you must get them quickly. Which event is the most popular? Do you give away all your tickets?

Look online for the price of a ticket to your event. Is it a lot of money? Tell the class.

A South African woman kisses her tickets to a World Cup soccer match.

THINK ABOUT THE PHOTO

Examine the photo. Look at the photo on the next page. Check (✓) all of the things below that you can find. Add a few words of your own to the list.

☐ smiles   ☐ camera   ☐ baseball cap   ☐ light sticks   ☐ red hair

☐ banner   ☐ crowd   _____   _____   _____

DISCUSSION

A. Discuss with a partner. This photo shows people in Tokyo, Japan, celebrating. Why do you think everyone is so happy?

B. Look and guess. Look at the photo again.

Student A: Find someone in the photo and describe him or her.

Student B: Find the person your partner is describing.

He is holding a pink and white banner.

Is this him?

Yes, it is.

CAPTION COMPETITION

What do you think the woman is saying to her friend? Tell a partner.

中川翔子@mixiコミュニティー
ギ・サ四国！
高知 徳島

Happy sports fans in Tokyo

Review 1

A. Complete the sentences. Complete each sentence with one of the missing words.

do	go	billion	hard	married

1. 1.35 _____ people live in China.
2. My friend got _____ last week.
3. It's a beautiful day, so let's _____ swimming.
4. I _____ karate on the weekends.
5. This homework is really _____ .

B. Complete these statements with your own ideas. Then share your ideas with a partner.

1. _____ (**is** / **are**) famous.
2. _____ (**is** / **are**) beautiful.
3. _____ (**is** / **are**) difficult.
4. _____ (**is** / **are**) crowded.
5. _____ (**is** / **are**) amazing.

C. Which country is it? Read the description. What country is each speaker talking about?

1. This country is in Asia. 127 million people live here. The capital city is Tokyo.

   The country is _____ .

2. This country is in South America. People speak Spanish. The capital city is Buenos Aires.

   The country is _____ .

3. This country is in Europe and Asia. 143 million people live here. The capital city is Moscow.

   The country is _____ .

Choose a country. Write a short description and ask your partner to guess which country it is.

D. Practice the conversation. Complete the conversation with the missing words. Then practice with a partner. Continue the conversation with your own ideas.

do	play	Brazil	crowded	city

A: So, where are you from?

B: I'm from _____ .

A: Really? Do you live in a _____ ?

B: Yes, I live in Rio de Janeiro.

A: Is it _____ ?

B: Yes. There are always a lot of people around.

A: What do you _____ ?

B: I _____ soccer for a famous team.

A: Wow. I'm really into soccer.

B: So, how about you?

The Night

Japanese capsule hotels are popular with businesspeople staying in a city for one night.

4097

4099

4096

WARM UP

Answer these questions with a partner.

1. Look at the picture. Would you like to sleep in a place like this?

2. Are you a "morning person" or a "night person"? Why?

3. What is your favorite day of the week? Which day(s) don't you like?

Nightlife

Days: _____ day **Time:** _____ day

A night market in Keelung, Taiwan: Thursday, 10:45 p.m.

Day: _____ **Time:** The first movie starts at _____ .

An outdoor movie theater in Baghdad, Iraq: 9:15 p.m.

LISTENING

A. Complete the survey. What can you do in your city or town at night? Check your ideas.

☐ go dancing at a club   ☐ go out to eat   ☐ go to karaoke
☐ go shopping   ☐ go to a movie   ☐ other: _____

Track 1-13 **B. Listen for gist.** Listen and number the pictures **1** to **3**.

Track 1-14 **C. Listen for days and times.** When is each place open? Write the days and times. Check answers with a partner.

D. Work with a partner. What do you like to do at night?

> Sometimes, I go out on Saturday night with friends. We go . . .

CONVERSATION

Track 1-15 **A. Listen to the conversation.**

A: I want to do something fun <u>on Saturday night</u>.

tonight
on Friday night
tomorrow night

B: Like what?

A: I don't know. Where's a good place to <u>go dancing</u>?

go out to eat
go to a movie
go shopping

B: <u>Club Yo-Yo</u> is good. It's open <u>from 7:00 to 3:00 a.m.</u> <u>on the weekend</u>.

Valentino's / from 6:30 on weekdays.
The Odeon Cinema / all night on the weekend
Central Mall / until 10 o'clock every night

A: That's perfect!

B. Practice with a partner. Use the words on the right.

C. Practice again. Talk about places you know.

Days: Tuesday to _____   **Time:** from _____
                                        to _____ a.m.

A nightclub in Paris, France: Sunday, 1:00 a.m.

READING

A. Vocabulary. Read the first paragraph. Then complete the chart below with a word in **blue**.

Words with opposite meanings			
awake ←——→ **asleep**		←——→ **sleepy**	
late ←——→		**go to bed** ←——→	

B. Prediction. Read statements **1–4**. Guess: Are they **true** or **false**?

	True	False
1. Most teenagers (people 13–19) are early birds.	——	——
2. Most teens sleep enough.	——	——
3. Night owls are more energetic in the morning than early birds.	——	——
4. More night owls get good grades in school.	——	——

EARLY BIRD OR NIGHT OWL?

Everyone has a natural sleep routine. You **go to bed** and **wake up** at a certain time. But everyone's routine is not the same. Some people—the early birds—go to bed **early** at night (around 9:00 or 10:00 p.m.). In the morning, they wake up easily and are **energetic**. Others—the night owls—stay **awake late** (until midnight or later). For them, it is difficult to wake up early.

What do we know about early birds and night owls? Here is what studies show.

- Teenagers are natural night owls. Also, most need nine to ten hours sleep a night. But in many places, the school or work day starts at 9:00 a.m. For this reason, only one in five teenagers sleeps enough.

- More early birds get good grades in school, but night owls do better on some intelligence (IQ) tests, according to a study of 1,000 Spanish teens. People with high scores on these tests usually get good jobs.

C. Read. Check your answers in **B**.

Track 1-16

D. Discuss with a partner. Are you an early bird or a night owl? What is good about being an early bird or a night owl?

LISTENING

A. Predict. What things are good (**G**) or bad (**B**) for sleep? Write **G** or **B** below.

_____ eating bananas	_____ reading in bed
_____ playing video games at night	_____ sleeping in the afternoon
_____ watching TV or movies in bed	_____ exercising before bed

 B. Listen for details. Check your answers in **A**. Which activity did the speaker NOT talk about? Circle it.

Track 1-17

C. Talk with a partner. Are any of the answers in **B** surprising?

Looking at screens is bad for sleep, say scientists.

DISCUSSION

Talking about how often you do things. Ask your partner about his or her sleep habits. **Use the questions on page 114.** Use the language below. Does your partner have good sleep habits? If not, what can he or she do differently?

> Do you sleep eight to nine hours a night?

> Yes, I do. I always go to bed at 10:00 and wake up at 6:00.

> No, I don't. I usually sleep for only five hours. I have a lot of homework!

35

Sleepwalking

One in ten people sleepwalk
in their lives, say scientists.

BEFORE YOU WATCH

About the video. The video talks about sleepwalking. When people sleepwalk, they are asleep but they get out of bed and walk around.

Prediction. Read **About the video**. What do you think is the main cause of sleepwalking? Circle your idea.

a. drinking coffee   b. not sleeping enough   c. stress

WHILE YOU WATCH

A. Watch the video. Check your answer on page 36.

B. What do you remember? Are these statements true or false? Check **True** or **False**, then watch and check your answers. Correct the false sentences.

	True	False
1. A sleepwalker is usually dreaming.	____	____
2. A person sleepwalks because a part of the brain "wakes up."	____	____
3. Some sleepwalkers eat and drink.	____	____
4. Most sleepwalkers can remember their actions.	____	____
5. Most sleepwalkers are adults.	____	____
6. It's difficult to wake up a sleepwalker.	____	____
7. It's best to wake up a sleepwalker.	____	____

AFTER YOU WATCH

A. Complete the sentences about yourself.

	Always	Usually	Sometimes	Never
1. I walk in my sleep.				
2. I talk in my sleep.				
3. I remember my dreams.				
4. I have nightmares (bad dreams).				

B. Work with a partner. Talk about your answers in **A** together.

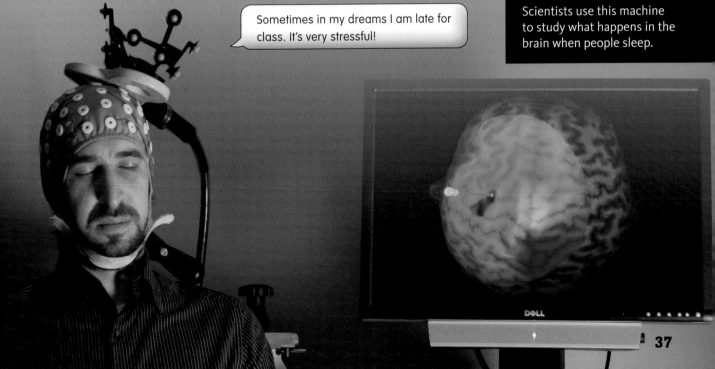

Sometimes in my dreams I am late for class. It's very stressful!

Scientists use this machine to study what happens in the brain when people sleep.

37

THE NIGHT SHIFT

You are going to talk about jobs that people do at night.

A. Choose a job. Working alone, choose one of these night jobs, or think of one of your own.

call center worker	hotel clerk	waiter or waitress	nurse	police officer
radio DJ	taxi driver	TV news anchor	other: _____	

B. Research the job. Imagine you do this job. What is a typical day like for you? Make a schedule. Write your daily activities and the times you do them. Think about these questions:

- When do you usually wake up?
- When do you start work? When do you finish?
- What do you do after work?

- When do you go to sleep?
- What is good about your night job? What's hard?

C. Interview a partner. Talk about your routine. Your partner will take notes and ask you questions. Take turns with different partners.

> Do you like your job?

> Sometimes. It's hard. I'm always sleepy. But the money is good.

D. Compare different jobs. With a partner, list the jobs you learned about in **B** and **C**. Then explain:

1. What are the good things about these night jobs? What are the bad things?
2. Which night job is the best? Which is the worst?

Look online at a video site. Can you find any interviews with night workers talking about their jobs?

This taxi driver in Madrid, Spain, works at night.

Fashion

A model at a British fashion show

WARM UP

Answer these questions with a partner.

1. Look at the photo. Do you like this style?

2. What are three fashionable cities around the world?

3. How many colors and items of clothing can you name? Make two lists.

GLOBAL FASHION

LONDON

TOKYO

NEW YORK

40

LISTENING

A. Understanding vocabulary. What are the people wearing? Label the photos using the words in the box.

boots	cap	coat	handbag	jeans	pants
scarf	shirt	T-shirt	shoes	skirt	suit

B. Listen for clothing. Listen and check your answers.

C. Listen for details. Circle the correct answers.

1. In this area of London, many people dress (**casually** / **stylishly**).
2. Hip hop fashion first came from (**New York** / **Sao Paulo**). It was first popular in the (**1980s** / **1990s**).
3. This style is originally from (**Japan** / **the U.K.**). People wear it (**to work** / **on weekends**).

D. Talk with a partner. Which clothing or styles do you like?

> I like the clothes in the Tokyo photo. I think they're really cool.

CONVERSATION

A. Listen to the conversation.

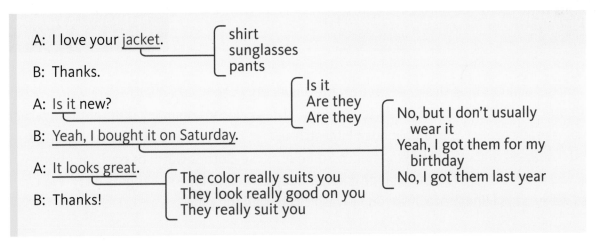

B. Practice with a partner. Use the words on the right.

C. Practice again. Talk about your partner's clothes.

READING

Track 1-21

A. Read. What types of clothing are talked about? Circle the clothes as you read.

scientist Juan Hinestroza

Matilda Ceesay wants to make anti-mosquito clothing more fashionable than this.

The Power Pocket uses body heat to charge your cell phone.

Scientists and clothing designers at Cornell University in the United States are working on fashion's next big thing: "wearable technology." These clothes do many different things, and some already exist. For example, Juan Hinestroza, a scientist from Colombia, is making shirts, pants, dresses, and other clothing items. Some of these clothes warm or cool your body when the weather changes. Others change color and style. A third type never gets dirty. We can use less water, says Hinestroza, if we don't wash clothes all the time.

Other scientists and designers are working together to protect people from malaria. Frederick Ochanda, a scientist from Kenya, is making a special suit to stop malaria. The clothes have a chemical inside that stops mosquitoes. Matilda Ceesay, a clothing designer from Gambia, is working with Ochanda to make the suit fashionable. This is important, she says, because the clothes must look good or no one will buy and wear them. Scientists need to work with fashion designers so the clothes are both comfortable and stylish.

B. Reading comprehension. What do these clothes do? Write your answers on the lines.

1. The Power Pocket _____

2. Juan Hinestroza's clothes **a.** _____

    b. _____ **c.** _____

3. Ceesay and Ochanda's special suit _____

C. Discuss with a partner. In your opinion, which item in the reading passage is the most helpful? Why?

> I like the Power Pocket. I always forget to charge my phone.

LISTENING

Track 1-22 **A. Listen for the main idea.** What are the speakers talking about? Check (✓) the correct photo.

Track 1-23 **B. Listen for details.** Choose the correct answer.

1. What can you NOT do with the item?

    a. take photos and video   b. talk on the phone   c. surf the Web

2. What does the woman say about the item?

    a. It's very stylish.   b. It's comfortable.   c. She doesn't want to wear it.

3. Does the man like the item?

    a. yes   b. no   c. He doesn't say.

DISCUSSION

Talking about clothing styles. Choose clothes from this unit. Do you like or dislike them? Explain to your partner. Use the language below and **on page 116.**

> I like the woman's dress. It's casual but stylish.

> I don't like the glasses. I think they look kind of weird.

Brass Rings

A Padaung woman shows a photo of herself without her neck rings.

BEFORE YOU WATCH

About the video. In Thailand, there is a group of people called the Padaung. The women wear special **neck rings**. Their necks look very long. In the video, there is a Padaung woman named Mabang. She is 19 years old.

Prediction. Read **About the video**. Which of these sentences about Padaung women do you think is true?

a. They only wear the brass rings for special occasions.

b. They wear the rings during the day, but take them off when they sleep at night.

c. They wear the rings all the time and only very rarely take them off.

WHILE YOU WATCH

A. Watch the video. Check your answer in **Before You Watch** on page 44. Are the statements below **true** or **false**?

	True	False
1. A girl first wears the rings at age 15.	——	——
2. The rings are comfortable.	——	——
3. In Padaung culture, a long neck is beautiful.	——	——
4. The rings are heavy.	——	——
5. To some foreigners, the neck rings are strange.	——	——
6. Women take off the rings to sleep and wash.	——	——
7. Mabang is happy to take off her neck rings.	——	——

B. Watch again. Check your answers in **A**. Then correct the false sentences.

AFTER YOU WATCH

Work with a partner. Answer the questions.

1. What do you think of the women's neck rings?

> I like the rings. They look interesting.

> I think they look uncomfortable!

2. Look at the pictures below. What do you think of these styles? Do you ever . . . ?

wear makeup	wear earrings or other jewelry	wear cologne or perfume
shave	use hair gel, mousse, or color	wear contact lenses

> Sometimes I wear hair gel on weekends, but I don't wear it to work.

In parts of Papua New Guinea, men wear makeup and fix their hair in special ways.

An Indian woman's jewelry and painted hands

A man with hair gel in his hair and wearing earrings

A FASHION SHOW & Survey

You are going to have a fashion show.

A. Make notes. Work with a partner. What clothes, shoes, and accessories is your partner wearing? Make a list.

B. Have a fashion show. Join other pairs to make a group of six. Your group is going to have a fashion show. Each pair in the group does this:

- **Person A:** Stand and walk around.
- **Person B:** What is your partner wearing? Tell the group.
- **Other students:** Say something nice about the clothes the person is wearing. Change roles and repeat.

C. Make a list. What clothing, colors, and accessories are the most common in your group? Make a list and write your answers on the board.

D. Discuss in groups. Answer these questions.

1. Read the answers on the board. In your class, what styles are most popular?
2. What do you think of these styles? Do you like them? Why or why not?

Look for videos of fashion shows on the Internet to see how models walk and show their clothing.

Models at a fashion show in London, U.K.

THINK ABOUT THE PHOTO

A. Prediction. Look at the photo on the next page. Where do you think the photographer took it?

  a. at the circus   b. at a parade   c. at a costume party   d. in a theater

B. Examine the photo. Look at the photo again. Check (✓) all of the things below that you can find. Add a few words of your own to the list.

☐ costumes   ☐ masks   ☐ lights   ☐ spectators

☐ hats   _____   _____   _____

DISCUSSION

A. Describe the photo. Take turns describing the photo to each other.

> The people look very tall.

> They are wearing silver masks.

B. Look at the photo again. This photo shows performers dancing on stilts during the Chingay Parade in Singapore (search for more information about the Chingay Parade online).

Imagine you can interview one of the performers. What questions will you ask? Make a list.

C. Interview a partner. Take turns as interviewer and performer and interview each other.

CAPTION COMPETITION

What do you think the performer is thinking? Tell a partner.

Performers in costume in
Singapore

Review 2

A. Match opposites. Draw lines to match the words on the left with their opposites. Then make your own sentences using these words and share them with your partner.

1. weekends   •   •   a. get up

2. go out   •   •   b. looks weird

3. go to bed   •   •   c. weekdays

4. suits you   •   •   d. cool

5. warm   •   •   e. stay home

B. Complete the sentences. Choose the correct answer in each sentence.

1. I'm really tired today because I (**woke up** / **stayed awake**) late last night.

2. I have lots of energy in the morning. I'm (**an early bird** / **a night owl**).

3. I put my money, keys, and make-up in my (**handbag** / **scarf**).

4. In winter, I wear these (**pants** / **boots**) on my feet.

5. I never wear a suit, shirt, or tie. I like to dress (**stylishly** / **casually**).

C. Write and share sentences. Write five sentences about what you like to do at night. Share your sentences with a partner.

D. Guess the clothes. Work with a partner. Think of an item of clothing. Describe it to your partner and have him or her guess what it is. Take turns.

> I wear it on my head.

> Is it a hat?

> No, but it's like a hat. I wear it when it's sunny.

> Is it a baseball cap?

> Yes, it is.

E. Complete the survey. Complete the sentences with your own ideas. Then interview a partner.

1. What do you like to do _____ ?

2. What time do you usually _____ ?

3. What is _____ wearing in class today?

4. Do you think _____ is stylish?

Homes

Colorful houses beside the water in Veneto, Italy

5

WARM UP

Answer these questions with a partner.

1. Look at the photo. Do you like these homes?
2. Do you live in a house or an apartment?
3. What's better: a big house in the country, or a small apartment in the city? Why?

Four Similar Apartments

LISTENING

A. Understand vocabulary. Look at the photos and the floor plan of the apartments in Seoul.

1. Which room are the families in? _____

2. Label the pictures with the items in the box.

blinds	cabinet	chair	computer	curtains	floor
lamp	picture	rug	sofa	wall	glass door

 Track 1-24 **B. Listen for gist.** Look at the photos. Number the apartments (**1–4**) as the speaker describes them.

 Track 1-24 **C. Listen for details.** Match each apartment with the correct sentence.

Description	Apartment			
1. The living room is very different from the others.	1	2	3	4
2. The family likes to travel.	1	2	3	4
3. There's a nice view from the balcony.	1	2	3	4
4. The family likes to play sports.	1	2	3	4

D. Work with a partner. Choose a photo. Say one thing about it. Your partner guesses the apartment.

> In this apartment, there are two pictures on the wall and there's a rug on the floor. Also . . .

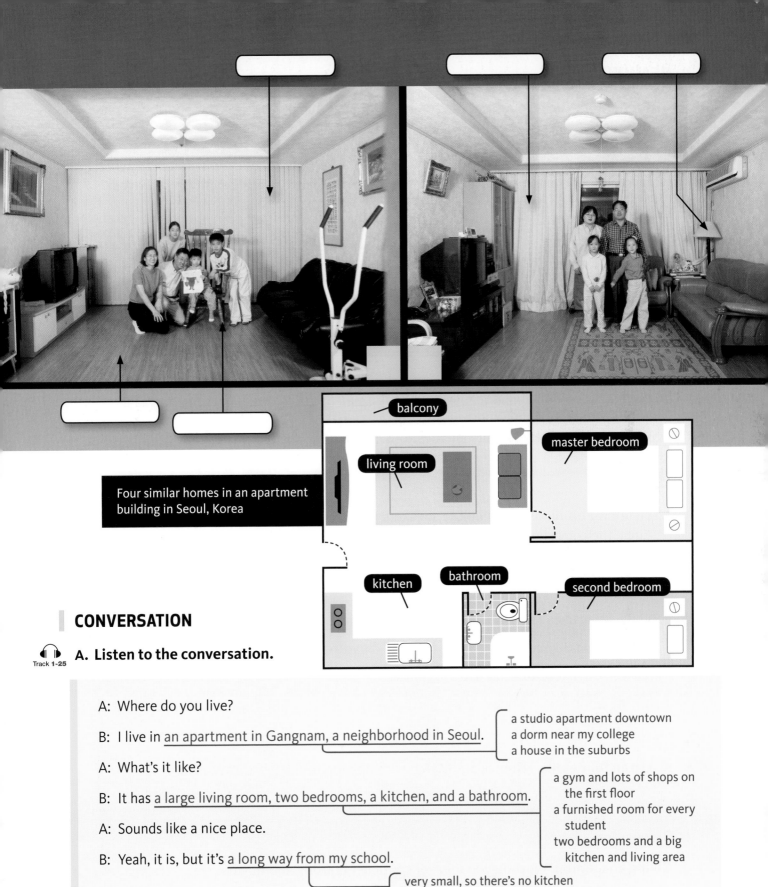

Four similar homes in an apartment building in Seoul, Korea

balcony

living room

master bedroom

kitchen

bathroom

second bedroom

CONVERSATION

🎧 **A. Listen to the conversation.**

Track 1-25

A: Where do you live?

B: I live in <u>an apartment in Gangnam, a neighborhood in Seoul</u>.

- a studio apartment downtown
- a dorm near my college
- a house in the suburbs

A: What's it like?

B: It has <u>a large living room, two bedrooms, a kitchen, and a bathroom</u>.

- a gym and lots of shops on the first floor
- a furnished room for every student
- two bedrooms and a big kitchen and living area

A: Sounds like a nice place.

B: Yeah, it is, but it's <u>a long way from my school</u>.

- very small, so there's no kitchen
- kind of noisy sometimes
- a long way from the station

B. Practice with a partner. Use the words on the right.

C. Practice again. Talk about your home.

53

READING

A. Prediction. The reading passages on the next page and on page 117 talk about two kinds of houses. Look at the pictures. How are the two homes similar?

B. Split reading. Student A: Read "Container Housing." Answer questions **1–4** in the chart below about container housing. **Student B: Turn to page 117 and read "Tiny Houses."**

	container housing	the tiny house
1. How big is it?		
2. How many rooms are there?		
3. Is it expensive?		
4. In your opinion, how many people can live in it?		

C. Work in pairs. Ask your partner questions to complete the rest of the chart.

LISTENING

A. Listen for opinions. What do the speakers think about each type of house? Circle the correct opinion.

Opinion	Reason
1. The man **likes / doesn't like** container apartments.	a. They're ugly.
2. The woman **likes / doesn't like** container apartments.	b. They save water and energy.
3. The man **likes / doesn't like** tiny houses.	c. They're too small.
4. The woman **likes / doesn't like** tiny houses.	d. They're comfortable.

B. Listen for details. Listen again. Match each opinion to the person's reason.

Discussion

Giving an opinion. What do you think of container housing and tiny houses? Use the language below.

> I like the tiny houses. I think they're cool.

> Yeah, I know. I like them, too.

> Really? I think they're too small.

LIVING SMALL

Today, 50% of the people on Earth live in cities. By 2030, it will be 60%. With more people in cities, there is less space, and housing costs more. What can we do? Here's an idea.

CONTAINER HOUSING

The city of Amsterdam is using old shipping containers as housing for students and other people. The containers are small—30 square meters (320 square feet)—but they are comfortable. There is space for a living area, bedroom, kitchen, and bathroom. These houses are also inexpensive: only a few thousand dollars to buy. Today, the containers are used around the world as homes and student dormitories, as well as shops, offices, and hotels.

A student relaxes in his container apartment.

In Amsterdam, the Netherlands, shipping containers are turned into homes for students.

Colorado, U.S.A.

ECO-FRIENDLY HOME

This **eco-friendly** home uses solar panels. These panels make **electricity** from the sun.

BEFORE YOU WATCH

About the video. In our homes, many electronic devices (like computers and TVs) and appliances (like microwave ovens and refrigerators) **waste** a lot of energy. Amory Lovin teaches people to **save** energy in their home. In the video, he visits the Cohen family's house.

A. Vocabulary matching. Read **About the video** and the photo caption. Then complete the sentences below using the words in **blue**.

1. We need _____ to power things like TVs, computers, and other electronics.
2. If something is _____ (or "green"), it is good for the Earth.
3. If you leave lights on when you leave a room, you _____ energy.
4. One way to _____ energy is to turn off lights.

B. Vocabulary completion. Choose the correct words to complete the sentences below.

How to charge a cell phone.

1. First (**turn on** / **turn off**) the power.
2. Then (**unplug** / **plug in**) the phone.
3. After it's charged, (**plug in** / **unplug**) the phone.
4. When you're finished, (**turn on** / **turn off**) the power.

WHILE YOU WATCH

A. Watch the video. Circle the correct answer in each sentence.

The Cohen family's home . . .	Amory Lovin's home . . .
1. is in the (**city** / **suburbs** / **mountains**).	4. is in the (**city** / **suburbs** / **mountains**).
2. (**wastes** / **saves**) a lot of energy.	5. (**wastes** / **doesn't waste**) a lot of energy.
3. has (**many** / **very few**) appliances and electronics.	6. uses (**no electricity** / **only solar power**).
Energy-saving tip	
7. To save energy at home, (**unplug** / **turn off**) appliances and electronics.	

B. Watch again. Read the sentences. Then listen and write a number.

1. In the U.S., houses and buildings use _____% of all energy.

2. The Cohen's TV is off, but it still uses energy. So each year, they pay $ _____ extra.

3. Lovin's whole house uses only _____ watts of electricity—a little more than turning on one light bulb.

AFTER YOU WATCH

A. Interview a partner. Ask him or her the questions below. Answer his or her questions.

1. How many appliances or electronics are there in your kitchen? Living area? Bedroom?

2. Are they plugged in at night?

3. Do you turn off the lights when you leave a room?

B. Review your answers in A. Answer the questions together.

1. Whose home uses more energy—yours or your partner's?

2. How can you make your homes more eco-friendly?

Change a regular light bulb to an eco-friendly light bulb and save energy.

Present a **green** home

You and your partner are architects. You are going to design and present an eco-friendly house.

A. Think about the house. Work with a partner. Answer the questions below.

1. What kind of house is it: a tree house, an underground house, a tiny house, a container house, a suburban house, an apartment, or something else?

2. How is the home eco-friendly? Use two or three ideas in your home.

> It has solar panels.   It has a vegetable garden.   It recycles water.
>
> It's small.   It has big windows for natural light.   _____

B. Design the house. Work in pairs. Draw a floor plan for the green house. Use the information in **A**. **See page 118 for ideas.**

C. Present your plan. Work with two other pairs. Take turns explaining your design to the others. Tell them how your house is green.

D. Choose a plan. In your group of six, choose the best plan.

Search online for information about or pictures of other green homes.

A green roof decreases energy costs for this house in London, England.

Buying & Selling

Nanjing Road in Shanghai, China, is one of the world's busiest shopping streets.

Dubai
Shopping Tour

Dubai

A woman shops for gold jewelry at the Gold Souk.

Traditional shoes at the Covered Souk

Sellers at the Spice Souk

LISTENING

A. Vocabulary. Look at the photos and read the information below.

A souk is a large marketplace in the Middle East and North Africa. At a souk, there are many shops. The city of Dubai, in the United Arab Emirates, has many souks. They are popular with both locals, shopping for food or clothing, and tourists looking for **souvenirs** to take home. In many souks, you must **bargain** to get the best price.

Are the sentences below **true** or **false**?

	True	False
1. A **souvenir** is something you buy and bring home from a trip.	_____	_____
2. If you **bargain** for something, you pay the price written on the item.	_____	_____

 Track 2-01
B. Listen for details. Number the photos **1–3** in the order the speaker talks about them.

 Track 2-02
C. Listen for details. Match each souk with one or two sentences.

The Covered Souk ●   ● There are hundreds of shops here.

The Gold Souk ●   ● Shop owners let you try the items.

The Spice Souk ●   ● You can buy souvenirs here.

     ● It is important to bargain here.

D. Work with a partner. Which souk would you like to visit? Why?

> I'd like to visit the Gold Souk because I love gold jewelry.

Conversation

 Track 2-03
A. Listen to the conversation.

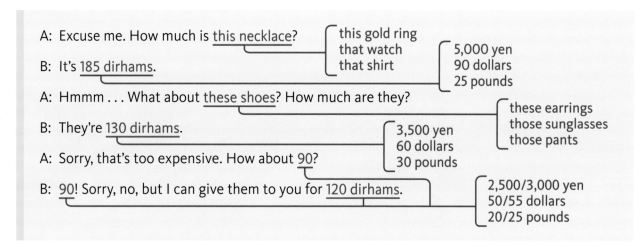

A: Excuse me. How much is <u>this necklace</u>?   [this gold ring / that watch / that shirt]   [5,000 yen / 90 dollars / 25 pounds]

B: It's <u>185 dirhams</u>.

A: Hmmm . . . What about <u>these shoes</u>? How much are they?   [these earrings / those sunglasses / those pants]

B: They're <u>130 dirhams</u>.   [3,500 yen / 60 dollars / 30 pounds]

A: Sorry, that's too expensive. How about <u>90</u>?

B: <u>90</u>! Sorry, no, but I can give them to you for <u>120 dirhams</u>.   [2,500/3,000 yen / 50/55 dollars / 20/25 pounds]

B. Practice with a partner. Use the words on the right.

C. Practice again. Make up your own items and prices.

READING

A. Prediction. Look at the photos and read the title and first paragraph of the reading passage. What is this article about?

a. Why people like to shop
b. How stores make people want to buy things

The Psychology of Selling

Do you ever go shopping for one thing, and then buy other things you don't need? Lots of people do. In fact, many stores use certain techniques so we buy more. Here's how:

1. **Bright colors:** Red, green, yellow—on a wall or a sign—make you stop and look at something.

2. **Time limits:** At some store sales, you have only a short time to buy something: *TODAY only: all T-shirts 25% off*. When you read this sign, you may be more likely to buy a shirt you don't need. Why? Because you can only get the lower price *today*.

3. **Special extras:** Other stores offer something special: *Buy one bag, get one 50% off!* When people read this sign, many will buy two bags instead of one. They may not need the second bag, but they buy it anyway.

4. **Free samples:** Some stores give shoppers a little food, drink, or other item to try for free. Studies show that when you try something, you are more likely to buy it.

The next time you go into a store or shop online, look around. How many of these techniques do you see?

B. Read and match. Read the passage. Then match each technique to its purpose.

Technique	Purpose
1. bright colors ●	● a. make you want to buy more than you need
2. time limits ●	● b. make you want to try something
3. special extras ●	● c. make you want to buy something quickly
4. free samples ●	● d. make you stop and look

C. Reading comprehension. Look at the photos on page 62. What technique(s) can you see? Write the number(s) (**1–4**) on the photos. Then share your answers with a partner.

D. Discuss with a partner. Do you ever see these techniques used in stores?

LISTENING

A. Listen for gist. What are the people talking about? Number the pictures **1–3** in order.

B. Listen for details. Listen again and circle the correct answers below.

Item	Will the person buy it?	Why?
1	Yes / No	a. She has a coupon so it's free. b. The man doesn't like it.
2	Yes / No	a. You must buy two. b. If you buy one, the second is 50% off.
3	Yes / No	a. There's a sale. b. It's expensive.

DISCUSSION

Asking about shopping habits. Ask your partner questions about his or her shopping habits. If your partner says yes, ask one more question. Use the language below.

Do you ever buy things you don't need?

What do you buy?

Yeah, sometimes.

Shoes. I have fifteen pairs in my closet!

THE FEZ SOUK

Customers shop for carpets at a souk in Morocco.

Fez, Morocco

BEFORE YOU WATCH

About the video. Fez is a city in Morocco. It has a famous souk. Vendors (sellers) here sell many different items. And every year, tourists from all over the world visit the souk.

Prediction. Guess: Are the statements below about Fez's souk **true** or **false**?

	True	False
1. It's a new shopping area in the city.	____	____
2. You must bargain.	____	____
3. Tourists often pay more for items than locals.	____	____
4. It's easy to buy too much here.	____	____

WHILE YOU WATCH

A. Watch the video. Check your answers above. Then correct the false sentences.

B. Watch the video again with the sound off. What things can you buy in the souk?
Check (✓) the things you see.

☐ birds   ☐ clothes   ☐ hats   ☐ sandals
☐ carpets   ☐ computers   ☐ jewelry   ☐ spices
☐ cell phones ☐ eggs   ☐ metal tables   ☐ watches

C. Watch again with the sound on. Check your answers in **B**.

AFTER YOU WATCH

A. Work with a partner. A student from another country is visiting your city for two weeks.
He or she wants to go shopping for the things in the chart below. Plan a one-day shopping
tour. Write your ideas.

	clothes	interesting souvenirs	a typical food or drink from your city or country
Marketplace or store name			
What can you buy?			
Expensive or inexpensive?			
Do you bargain?			

B. Work with another pair. Explain your plan. Then listen to theirs. Do you like the other
pair's ideas? Why or why not?

> The first stop on our shopping tour is an outdoor market. This place sells . . .

Fruit and vegetables on sale at
an outdoor market in Morocco

65

SELL A PRODUCT

You are going to sell something to your classmates.

A. Choose something to sell. Work with a partner. You work in a large shopping mall. You want people to come into your store and buy things. Think of something to sell. Give it a price.

| Item _____ | Price _____ |

B. Make a poster to sell your item. In your poster, use techniques from the reading on page 62. You can also use photos, music, and coupons to sell your item.

C. Prepare your store. Put your poster on the wall. Put the product you are selling on a desk.

D. Divide the class into shoppers and store clerks. Shoppers: You have $200 to spend. Visit the different stores. Buy things with your money. **Store clerks:** You want to sell a lot. When you sell an item, write the item's name and price on a small piece of paper. Give it to the shopper.

E. Choose the most successful store. Which store sold the most items? Which store made the most money?

Look online for photos of your product or music to play in your store.

Istanbul Cevahir Shopping and Entertainment Center is one of the largest shopping malls in the world.

THINK ABOUT THE PHOTO

A. Examine the photo. Look at the photo on the next page. Check all of the things below that you can find. Add a few words of your own to the list.

☐ people ☐ mannequin ☐ shopping cart ☐ bicycle ☐ flag

☐ building ☐ car _____ _____ _____

B. Learn about the photo. Complete the description of the photo by choosing the correct words.

People are (**standing** / **sitting**) under an upside-down shopping cart outside the European Union headquarters in Brussels, Belgium. The people want shoppers to think carefully about the things they (**buy** / **sell**). Some shoppers buy things at very (**cheap** / **expensive**) prices. However, workers from poor countries often make these things. The workers often work (**long** / **short**) hours for (**very little** / **a lot of**) money.

DISCUSSION

A. Describe the photo. Work with a partner. Take turns describing the photo to each other.

> There are three mannequins.

B. Talk with a partner. The people in the photo want shoppers to think about what they buy. Talk about the things you buy.

1. What kinds of things do you buy?

2. Do you think about who made them?

3. Would you pay more money for your shopping to help the workers?

C. Learn more online. On the Internet, find out about how the International Organization for Migration (IOM) helps workers.

CAPTION COMPETITION

What do you think this person is thinking?

People under a giant shopping cart in Brussels, Belgium.

Review 3

A. Vocabulary review. Complete each sentence using the words in the box.

> bargain   think   suburbs   souvenirs   try

1. I don't want to rent an apartment in the middle of the city. I want to live in the
   _____ .

2. I like living in the city. I _____ the countryside is too boring.

3. You went to Hawaii on vacation? Did you buy any _____ ?

4. In Australia, you don't have to _____ in stores—prices don't usually change.

5. Do you ever _____ free samples in stores?

B. Complete the sentences. Draw lines to match the two halves.

1. My house is great   •   •   a. because I have a big family.

2. I want to live in a tiny house   •   •   b. because you can buy cheap souvenirs there.

3. I need a large house   •   •   c. because they are easy to clean.

4. I like the night markets   •   •   d. because it is near a subway station.

5. I like shopping in January   •   •   e. because there are many sales then.

C. Complete each sentence with your own idea. Then share your ideas with a partner.
Does he or she agree with you?

1. _____ is/are modern.

2. _____ is/are ugly.

3. _____ is/are comfortable.

4. _____ is/are expensive.

> I think this coat is really comfortable.

> Yeah? It looks great on you, too.

D. Complete the survey. Complete the questions below with your own ideas.
Then interview a partner.

1. What do you think of _____ houses?

2. Do you want to live near a _____ ?

3. Do you ever buy _____ ?

4. Do you ever go shopping in _____ ?

Weather

People gather in the snow to vote in Appenzell-Innerrhoden, Switzerland.

WARM UP

Answer these questions with a partner.

1. How is the weather in the photo?

2. In your country, how many seasons are there?

3. Which season is your favorite? Why?

71

How's the weather?

Costa Rica

A wet footbridge over the rain forest in Costa Rica

LISTENING

A. Prediction. Look at the photos and read the fast facts.

1. a. What's the capital city of Costa Rica?
   b. Why is Costa Rica popular to visit?

2. Guess: How is the weather in Costa Rica?

Track 2-06

B. Listen for the main idea. Choose the best answer.

The speaker will mainly talk about _____ Costa Rica.

a. the wildlife in   b. the best time to visit   c. the history of

> ### Costa Rica Fast Facts
>
> - **Population:** 4.5 million
> - **Capital city:** San José
> - **Official language:** Spanish
> - **Highlights:**
>   - Its rain forests, animals, beautiful beaches, and mountains
>   - Its many outdoor activities

C. Listen for details. Complete the table below using the words in the box. Some words may be used more than once.

cloudy   cold   cooler   dry   hot   rains   sunny   warm

Months	How's the weather?
May–June	Mornings: It's _____ and _____. Afternoons and evenings: It _____, sometimes a lot.
July–August	West coast: It's _____ and _____; it _____ at night.
February–April	At the beach: It's _____ and _____. In San José: It's _____. In the mountains: It's _____ at night.

D. Discuss with a partner. In your opinion, when is the best time to visit Costa Rica? Use the information above.

> I think May or June is best. It rains more then, but prices are lower.

CONVERSATION

A. Listen to the conversation.

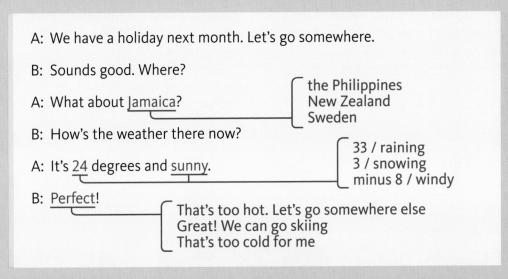

A: We have a holiday next month. Let's go somewhere.

B: Sounds good. Where?

A: What about Jamaica?
    the Philippines
    New Zealand
    Sweden

B: How's the weather there now?

A: It's 24 degrees and sunny.
    33 / raining
    3 / snowing
    minus 8 / windy

B: Perfect!
    That's too hot. Let's go somewhere else
    Great! We can go skiing
    That's too cold for me

B. Practice with a partner. Use the words on the right.

C. Practice again. Talk about other places.

A sunny beach in Puerto Viejo, Costa Rica

READING

A. Understand vocabulary. How do you feel in different kinds of weather? Complete the sentences below using the feelings in the box.

> calm   relaxed   cranky   energetic   happy   lazy   sad   blue   sleepy   tired

1. When it's **cold** and **cloudy**, I feel _____.
2. When it's **raining**, I feel _____.
3. When it's **sunny** and **warm**, I feel _____.
4. When it's **very hot**, I feel _____.

Track 2-09

B. Split reading. Student A: Read the passage below about warm weather.
Student B: Turn to page 120 and read about cold weather.

Sunshine and Happiness

Imagine a sunny, warm day. It's 24°C (75°F) and you're outside. How do you feel? For most people, the answer is "happy"—and there is a reason why. Warm, sunny weather relaxes our muscles and helps us feel calm. Also, when we are in the sun, a chemical called serotonin increases in our body. When serotonin increases, we feel awake and happier.

Now imagine a hot day; it's 32°C (90°F). In this weather, most people feel less happy. In the heat, our heart beats faster, but we think more slowly. For this reason, it is harder to be calm and think clearly. We also have less energy. In this weather, people often feel cranky and get angry easily. Others feel tired and lazy.

People relax in a park in London. Sunlight can make you happier, say scientists.

C. Work in pairs. Student A: Answer questions **1** and **2** below. Ask your partner questions to answer questions **3** and **4**.

1. On a sunny day, most people feel (**happy** / **lazy**) because warm, sunny weather (**relaxes us** / **makes us less energetic**).

2. On a hot day we think more (**quickly** / **slowly**), so it is (**easier** / **harder**) to think clearly.

3. On rainy days, some people are (**more** / **less**) energetic, so they (**work better** / **feel more lazy**).

4. On cloudy or rainy days, the amount of serotonin in our body (**increases** / **decreases**). This can make us feel (**tired or blue** / **happier and more energetic**).

D. Discuss with a partner. Are your answers in **A** and the information in the readings the same?

> On rainy days, I usually feel sad, because I can't go outside.

LISTENING

Track **2-11**

A. Listen for details. Read the ideas under **1** and **2**. Check the ideas you hear.

---

1. When it's hot . . .

☐ take a shower.
☐ eat some ice cream.
☐ have a cold drink.

2. On a cold winter's day . . .

☐ walk outside in the morning.
☐ have a hot drink.
☐ use a bright lamp.

Reasons

a. It makes you feel cooler.
b. Sunlight makes you feel happier.
c. It makes you feel warmer.
d. It increases your energy.
e. It's similar to sunlight.

Track **2-12**

B. Listen for details. Draw lines to match the ideas in **1** and **2** with reasons. One reason is extra.

C. Work with a partner. On a hot or cold day, what things in **A** do you do? What else do you do?

DISCUSSION

Asking how someone is. Student A: Imagine you have a problem with the weather. Tell your partner. **Student B:** Your partner seems unhappy. Ask how he or she is. Make a suggestion. Use the expressions on the right. **See page 121 for more ideas.**

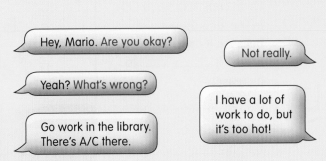

> Hey, Mario. Are you okay?

> Not really.

> Yeah? What's wrong?

> I have a lot of work to do, but it's too hot!

> Go work in the library. There's A/C there.

DEADLY HEATWAVE

A boy stays cool during a heatwave in Pakistan.

BEFORE YOU WATCH

France

About the video. A *heatwave* describes many days of very hot weather. Heatwaves can be dangerous: people can die, and fires can start. In 2003, there was a heatwave in Europe—one of the worst in modern history.

A. Understand vocabulary. Look at the diagram below. Complete the information using the words in the box.

> air   control   dangerous   temperature   water

Plants help 1. _____ CO_2 in the air and keep Earth cool. Too much CO_2 in the air is 2. _____ because it causes the Earth's 3. _____ to increase.

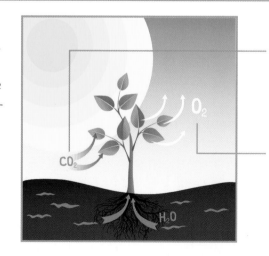

Plants take in carbon dioxide (CO_2) and 4. _____ (H_2O) from the environment.

Then plants release oxygen (O_2) into the 5. _____. Humans need oxygen to live.

WHILE YOU WATCH

A. Watch the video. Write numbers to complete the summary below.

In August 2003, Europe, particularly France, had one of its worst heatwaves ever. The temperature was sometimes more than 1. _____ degrees. Because of this, many people died. On one night, August 10th, between 2. _____ and 3. _____ people died. In total, more than 4. _____ people died in Europe, including 5. _____ in France.

B. Watch again. Check your answers in **A**. Then choose the correct answers to complete the information below.

Scientists noticed another bad thing that year. (**Carbon dioxide / Oxygen**) levels in the air above Paris were (**higher / lower**) than usual. Plants normally take in (**carbon dioxide / oxygen**) from the air, and release (**carbon dioxide / oxygen**). However, the extreme heat reversed this process. This meant that the plants were no longer cooling and cleaning the air as well.

AFTER YOU WATCH

A. Discussion. Work with a partner. Why is a heatwave (like the one in 2003) bad for our planet? Which of the things below are good to do in a heatwave? Which aren't?

drink water	go swimming	smoke	eat a big meal
go to the mall	turn off the lights	wear dark clothing	go outside
turn on a fan or the A/C	open your windows	exercise	wear sunscreen

B. Role play. Imagine there is a heatwave in your area. Make a 30-second radio or TV weather report. Talk about the weather and tell people ways to stay safe and cool. Use your ideas from **A**. Then show your weather report to another pair.

A boat stuck on a dry river during a heatwave in Serbia

I ♥ My City All Year

Make an advertisement to bring people to your city in different seasons.

A. Plan your campaign. Work with a partner. Your city council wants to increase the number of visitors to your city all year round. Discuss these questions.

1. How's the weather in each season in your city? List your ideas.

> In summer, the weather in Paris is usually pretty cool—about 24 degrees. But sometimes, it's also really hot. In July, it often rains, too.

2. What can people do in your city in the different seasons—when the weather is good and bad?

> When it's hot or raining, visitors can go to a museum. There's air conditioning.

> Yeah, and when it's warm, you can do a boat tour on the Seine. There's also a nice park . . .

B. Prepare an advertisement. Together, make a poster or video about the weather in different seasons. Talk about things tourists can do in your city. Also prepare a short presentation. Take turns so each person talks.

C. Present your ad to the class. Listen to the others. Then vote for the best one.

Use the Internet to find the opening hours and admission prices of the places in your poster.

Paris, France

Tourists take a boat tour on the Seine, Paris.

Mysteries

8

Two men took this photo of a monster in Loch Ness, Scotland, in 1934. Many years later, one of the men said that it was a fake.

WARM UP

Answer these questions with a partner.

1. Look at the photo. What do you know about the Loch Ness monster? Do you believe it exists?

2. Do you know any mysteries?

3. Do you believe there is life on other planets?

SCARY MONSTERS

Is this footprint, found near Mount Everest, from a Yeti?

The Himalaya mountains, Nepal. Does the Yeti live here?

WHAT IS THE YETI?

- There are stories about it in the Himalayan mountains. People see or hear it at night.
- It's half man, half animal. It kills animals and takes children.

LISTENING

Track **2-13**

A. Complete the information. Look at the photos and complete the information below using the past form of the words in the box. Then listen and check your answers.

| be | move | have | hear | not believe | see | hear | ~~be~~ |

Reinhold Messner is a famous mountain climber from Austria. He 1. _____*was*_____ the first person to climb the highest 14 mountains on Earth. For years, Messner 2. _____ stories about the Yeti, but he 3. _____ them. Then he 4. _____ a scary experience. He 5. _____ alone on a hike in the Himalayas. . . . Suddenly, he 6. _____ a strange sound, and he 7. _____ something—maybe an animal. It 8. _____ very fast . . .

B. Listen for details. Which animal looks most like Messner's description? Circle it. Then circle the correct word in statements **1–6**.

A

B

Messner said the Yeti . . .

1. walked on (**two** / **four**) legs.
2. had (**short** / **long**) legs.
3. was very (**tall** / **short**).
4. had (**long** / **short**) arms.
5. had (**very little** / **a lot of**) hair on its body.
6. walked very (**quickly** / **slowly**).

 Track 2-14

C. Listen for numbers. Read the summary. Then listen and write a number.

Today, there are no apes in the Himalayas. But in the past, there were.

Around 1. _____ years ago, a type of giant ape lived in the Himalayas.

It was 2. _____ meters (10 feet) tall and weighed more than

3. _____ kilograms (1,000 pounds). Some scientists think it walked on

4. _____ legs, like humans. Maybe the Yeti and this ancient (very old)

animal are similar.

D. Work with a partner. Scientists have a theory (idea) about the Yeti. What is it? What do you think the Yeti is?

> I think the Yeti is really a . . .

CONVERSATION

 Track 2-15

A. Listen to the conversation.

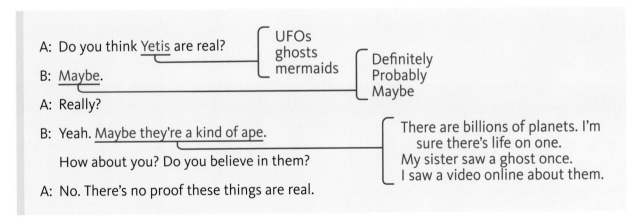

A: Do you think Yetis are real?

B: Maybe.

A: Really?

B: Yeah. Maybe they're a kind of ape.

 How about you? Do you believe in them?

A: No. There's no proof these things are real.

UFOs
ghosts
mermaids

Definitely
Probably
Maybe

There are billions of planets. I'm sure there's life on one.
My sister saw a ghost once.
I saw a video online about them.

B. Practice with a partner. Use the words on the right.

C. Practice again. Give your own opinions.

READING

Track 2-16

A. Work with a partner. Look at the photo and read the first part of the story. Then guess what happens next.

> a. Ehrman sees a UFO.   b. Ehrman gets a strange signal.   c. Ehrman finds a new planet.

B. Finish the passage. Turn to page 122. Read the rest of the story and check your idea in **A**. Then answer the questions on page 123.

The **Wow!** Signal
Did aliens try to contact us?

Jerry Ehman was a scientist. In 1977, he worked at Ohio State University in the U.S.

At the school, there was a large radio telescope called "Big Ear." It listened for signals from space, and it made a report each day.

Ehman read the report every day. Each time, the sky was quiet. Then, on August 15, something interesting happened.

Radio telescopes, like this one in the U.S., get signals from space.

A model of an alien body from Roswell. Today, a lot of tourists visit Roswell, New Mexico, in the U.S.

In the past, the U.S. military used objects like this one to study space.

LISTENING

Track 2-18

A. Listen for a sequence. In July 1947, something strange happened in Roswell, New Mexico. Read the sentences. Then listen and order the events from **1–5**.

_____ The army found pieces of a flying machine on the ground.

_____ People saw something flying in the night sky.

_____ The army said the machine was a weather balloon.

_____ People heard a loud crash.

_____ The army said the machine was a UFO from space.

Track 2-19
B. Listen for details. Circle the best answer.

1. Today, the army says the flying machine was definitely a _____ .
   a. UFO   b. weather balloon   c. small plane

2. In 1947, some people in Roswell saw _____ near the crash site.
   a. strange bodies   b. dead people   c. an old man

3. Chase Brandon worked for the government. He says _____ .
   a. there were no aliens   b. the flying machine wasn't from Earth   c. both a and b

4. Chase Brandon believes the events at Roswell _____ happened.
   a. definitely   b. probably   c. never

C. Work with a partner. What do you think happened at Roswell?

DISCUSSION

Telling a story. Work in a small group. Think of a story to tell. It can be real or made-up. Use the past tense and the expressions **on pages 123 and 124**. Your partners will ask you questions and guess: Is your story real or not?

> One night, I was home alone and there was a big storm.

> Were you scared?

> At first, no, but then . . .

83

WHAT KILLED THE DINOSAURS?

Chicxulub

Over 65 million years ago, an asteroid (a very large rock from space) **crashed** into the Earth near Chicxulub, Mexico. It cause the extinction (death) of the dinosaurs, scientists think.

BEFORE YOU WATCH

> **About the video.** An asteroid crashed into Earth. But why did the dinosaurs die? To answer this question, scientists use a small **bomb** to **recreate** the asteroid **explosion**.

A. Understand vocabulary. Look at the photo above. Read the caption and **About the video**. Then complete the sentences below using the words in **blue**.

1. When a large asteroid _____ into Earth, it caused a huge _____—more powerful than even the largest _____ made by humans.

2. If you _____ something, you make it exist or happen again.

B. Prediction. Why do scientists want to learn from the small bomb?

a. Are there any dinosaur bones in that area?

b. What happens during an explosion?

c. Is the original asteroid still under the ground?

WHILE YOU WATCH

A. Watch the video. Put the events in order from 1–**4**. Then check your answer(s) in B on page 84.

_____ Scientists see a large shockwave (a powerful wall of air).

_____ The bomb explodes.

_____ Scientists put a bomb in the ground.

_____ A lot of debris falls from the sky.

B. Watch again. Complete each sentence with a number or word.

65 million years ago, an asteroid crashed into Earth.

a. It was _____ kilometers wide.

b. It killed the dinosaurs and _____% of all other life.

c. It caused a shockwave that killed anything within _____ kilometers in _____ seconds.

d. It made a crater in Mexico that is _____ kilometers wide.

C. Talk with a partner. Tell a partner about your answers above.

AFTER YOU WATCH

A. Role play. Work in a group of four: two people are scientists and two are reporters.

Scientists: Prepare to talk to reporters about your experiment. Think about these questions: What did you do? What did you learn? What probably killed the dinosaurs? Use your answers above to explain.

Reporters: Think of 5 or 6 questions to ask the scientists. You want to learn about their experiment. Then take turns interviewing the scientists. Do their answers match the ideas in the video?

B. Work in a new group. This time, change roles.

Dinosaurs are extinct. Now scientists say 75% of Earth's species may be extinct in 300 years. Can you guess why?

What's your theory?

You will try to explain a mystery.

A. Choose a mystery. Work with a partner. Choose a mystery you are interested in. See the list below for ideas or use another mystery you know about.

Our mystery is _____.

> **A mysterious place:** e.g., Stonehenge, the Bermuda Triangle
>
> **A mysterious animal or person:** the Chupacabra, the Loch Ness monster
>
> **A mysterious event:** crop circles, the Mary Celeste

B. Research your topic. Think of a list of questions (*Who? What? When? Why? Where? How?*). Then find answers for them. What's your theory about the mystery?

> Where is Stonehenge?

> Why did people make it?

C. Prepare a short presentation. Make a poster or a slideshow to tell other people about your topic.

D. Present your mystery. Explain the mystery and your theory about it to a small group. Listeners, say what you think about the theory.

Look online to see what other people think is the answer to your mystery.

This crop circle appeared one night in a garden in England.

THINK ABOUT THE PHOTO

A. Examine the photo. Look at the photo on the next page. Check (✓) all of the things below that you can find. Add a few words of your own to the list.

- ☐ hotel
- ☐ land
- ☐ sky
- ☐ people
- ☐ northern lights
- ☐ electric lights
- ☐ lake
- ☐ _____

B. Learn about the photo. Complete the description of the photo by choosing the correct words.

The aurora borealis appears (**over** / **under**) a hotel in southern Iceland. The aurora borealis is also known as the (**northern** / **southern**) lights. Iceland's cool, (**clear** / **cloudy**) evenings make it easy for people to enjoy the amazing show in the (**lake** / **sky**). The beautiful lights are reflected in the (**lake** / **sky**).

DISCUSSION

A. Discuss with a partner. What do you like about the photo?

> I like the different colors of the lights.

B. Talk about other photos. Do an Internet search for photos of the northern lights. Find a photo you like. Show it to your partner and say why you like it.

C. Think about the photo. Would you like to stay at this hotel? Why or why not? Tell a partner.

D. Interview your classmates. Have you ever seen the northern lights? What are some amazing views you have seen?

CAPTION COMPETITION

What do you think these people are saying?

The aurora borealis, or northern lights, above a hotel in Iceland

Review 4

A. Vocabulary review. Complete the sentences using the words in the box.

> degrees   cranky   calm   scared   real

1. Many children believe that Santa Claus is _____.
2. I didn't sleep well last night, so I feel very _____ today.
3. I like to sit in the garden because it makes me feel _____.
4. Today is the hottest day of the year. It's around 37 _____.
5. I am _____ of flying because I don't think planes are safe.

B. True or false. Look back at Unit 7. Are the statements below **true** or **false**?

	True	False
1. The capital city of Costa Rica is San José.	____	____
2. People in Costa Rica speak English and Portuguese.	____	____
3. Sunny weather makes people feel blue.	____	____
4. On a cloudy day, you can use a bright lamp to feel better.	____	____
5. In Europe, there is a heatwave every summer.	____	____

C. Make a quiz. Now look back at Unit 8 and write some statements that are true and some that are false. Show your partner. Ask him or her to say whether they are true or false.

D. Talking about feelings. Complete the sentences below to say when you feel these emotions. Tell your partner about each one.

1. When _____, I feel cranky.
2. When _____, I feel lazy.
3. When _____, I feel relaxed.
4. When _____, I feel scared.
5. When _____, I feel angry.

> When I stay up late, I feel sleepy the next day.

9

Education

A student takes an exam at a school in Dubai.

WARM UP

Answer these questions with a partner.

1. How many different schools have you been to?
2. What is (or was) your favorite school subject?
3. What do you want to learn in the future?

The Power of Learning

A girl learns math at a school in east Africa. Worldwide, 61 million children don't go to school—60% are girls.

LISTENING

Track **2-20**

A. Listen for numbers. Read the information. Then listen and write the numbers.

Number of girls in school: Kenya

Elementary school (ages 6–13)

- _____% of all girls go
- Only _____ in 5 girls in poor areas go

High school (ages 14–18)

- Only _____% of all girls go; in poor areas only _____% go
- Families don't have money
- Girls leave school and get married at age _____ or _____

Three girls at ▶ Kakenya Ntaiya's school. Studies show that educated women make more money and their families have better lives.

B. Discuss with a partner. In your country, do most girls finish school?

C. Listen for details. Read these statements about Kakenya Ntaiya, a Kenyan woman. Then listen and put her story in order from **1** to **4**.

Track 2-21

_____ a. She went to college in the U.S.

_____ b. She returned to her village and started a school.

_____ c. She talked to her father.

_____ d. Her family wanted her to get married.

D. Discuss with a partner. Going to school changed Kakenya's life. How?

> She finished high school. Then she studied in the U.S. Later . . .

Kakenya Ntaiya opened a school for girls in Kenya. She wants all girls to get a good education.

CONVERSATION

A. Listen to the conversation.

Track 2-22

A: I'm going to <u>London</u> this summer.

New York City
Brazil
Rome

B: Really? On vacation?

A: No, to take <u>a business</u> class. In it, students learn <u>to give presentations and write in English</u>.

a fashion design / about fashion history
an earth science / about climate change
an Italian / to speak and read Italian

B: Interesting.

A: Yeah, and you can also <u>do an internship at a company</u>.

go to fashion shows
visit the Amazon
stay with a local family

B: That sounds great.

B. Practice with a partner. Use the words on the right.

C. Practice again. Use your imagination or talk about real overseas study programs.

READING

A. **Work with a partner.** Do you like to take photos? Are you a good photographer? Predict: What do you think students learn at a Photo Camp?

Track 2-23

B. **Read about Photo Camp.** As you read, check your prediction in **A**.

Photo Camp

Anyone can take a photo. But can you use a camera to tell a story, too?

What is it?

Photo Camp is a four-day class. Young adults learn to take photos and tell stories with their cameras. Their teachers are *National Geographic* photographers.

What happens?

Students have class in the morning. They learn things like this: *How can you take a beautiful photo of a person or something in nature? When is it good to take a black and white photo?* In the afternoon, they go out and take lots of pictures. Then they learn to choose the best ones.

Photo Camp students visited Barbados to take photos.

In some Photo Camp classes, students learn about problems in their area. For example, in the Caribbean country of Barbados, students learned about water problems. Then they took photos and wrote about it.

Photo Camps also bring people together. In one camp, students from Brazil visited Doha (Qatar's capital) for ten days. Together, the students traveled around Qatar. They learned about Qatar's culture and language. And they took some great pictures.

C. **Reading comprehension.** Take turns asking and answering the questions with a partner.

1. What do students learn at Photo Camp?
2. What do students do on a typical day at Photo Camp?
3. List two places that Photo Camps have visited.
4. What did students do in each of those places?

D. **Work in a small group.** What fun classes can you do in your area? Go online and find one. Tell the group about it. Choose one together.

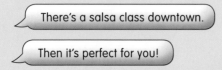

There's a salsa class downtown.

Then it's perfect for you!

But I can't dance.

LISTENING

Track 2-24 **A. Listen for details.** You will hear an interview about a special school program. Read the information. Then listen and circle the correct answers.

The Independent Project

The Independent Project was started by a high school student in the U.S. Different high schools across the U.S. now use the program. In it, every student learns to (**cook** / **do something new**). The students have four (**weeks** / **months**) to finish their project. At the end, they (**give a presentation** / **write an essay**) to explain their project.

Track 2-25 **B. Listen for details.** Read one student's project schedule. Write one word in each blank.

> My Project (Spring semester)
>
> Week 1: State my _____ clearly.
>
> • One idea: Learn to cook a meal for 80 people.
>
> Weeks 2–16:
>
> • Talk to _____ and other experts.
>
> • Read _____ and information on the _____.
>
> At the end: Show and explain the project to other _____.

C. Work with a partner. What do you think of the Independent Project? Would you like to do it in your school?

DISCUSSION

Talking about ability. Finish this sentence: *I want to learn to* _____ .
Try to find someone in class to teach you. Use the language below.

> Can you drive?

> Do you know how to drive?

> No, I can't. I never learned how.

> Yeah. I learned last year. I can teach you.

Learning Across Generations

Johannesburg, South Africa

A shantytown in South Africa

BEFORE YOU WATCH

About the video. Seventeen-year-old Mamorena Chaane and her mother Tandi live in South Africa. Tandi **grew up** in a shantytown (a very poor area) in Johannesburg. Today, life is better for the younger **generation**, but Tandi thinks it is important to remember the past.

A. Understand vocabulary. Read **About the video**. Then complete the sentences below using the words in **blue**.

1. Many people in the older _____ didn't go to college. They were too poor.

2. My dad _____ in Seoul. He lived there as a child and teenager.

B. Work with a partner. Answer the questions.

1. Who are Mamorena and Tandi Chaane?

2. How is life for many younger South Africans today?

96

WHILE YOU WATCH

A. Watch the video. Is each sentence about Mamorena or Tandi (her mother)? Check the box. Sometimes both answers are correct.

	Mamorena	Tandi
1. She goes to an expensive school.		
2. She used to be very poor.		
3. She is a successful businesswoman.		
4. She goes to Johannesburg every week.		
5. She lives in a nice house in the suburbs.		
6. She feels more Western than South African.		

B. Watch again. Tandi wants Mamorena to learn about South Africa's past. Is Mamorena interested in this? Why or why not? Discuss with a partner.

AFTER YOU WATCH

A. Work on your own. Think of someone older than you. Then, think about your answers to these two questions.

1. What can you learn from this person?
2. What can you teach this person?

B. Work in a small group. Talk about your answers in **A** together.

> My dad knows a lot about business. He can teach me to start my own company.

A boy walks past a poster of Nelson Mandela in Johannesburg, South Africa.

Student Tutors

You are going to teach other students how to do something.

A. What can you do? See the list below for ideas, or think of your own idea.

I can _____

I can . . . well.	Teach your group how to . . .
draw	draw a simple picture.
sing	sing a song. First, give your group the words. Then practice it with them.
cook a certain food	make this dish. Use photos to show each step.
play a game	play the game.
dance	do a simple dance.
speak another language	say three expressions in that language.
my idea: _____	

B. Prepare a short presentation. Think about how you can teach another student your skill. See the chart above for ideas.

Search for photos or videos on the Internet to help you teach your skill.

C. Teach your skill to other students. Work in a group of four. **Tutor:** Give your presentation. **Learners:** Listen and take notes. Follow the speaker's directions. Then change roles.

D. Practice your new skill. Choose a skill you learned in **C**. Teach a new partner how to do it.

Hi, everyone. My name is Jin Soo and I can speak French. I learned to speak it in high school. Later, I lived in France for three months. Today, I'm going to teach you three expressions in French. The first is . . .

A Japanese woman in London teaches a girl how to make an animal using origami.

10

Water

A long time with no rain has dried this reservoir in Texas, U.S.A.

WARM UP

Answer these questions with a partner.

1. Do you drink a lot of water?
2. How many different ways do you use water every day? Make a list.
3. How many liters (or gallons) of water do you use each day?

YOUR DRINKING WATER

Worldwide, people in the U.S. and Italy drink the most bottled water, followed by Mexico, China, and Brazil.

LISTENING

A. Predict. How much do you know about bottled water? Choose the correct answers in the first sentences of **1–5** below.

1. There are often (**fewer** / **more**) unhealthy chemicals in bottled water than in tap water. These chemicals come from the _____ in the bottles.

2. Most bottled water is (**cleaner than** / **the same as**) tap water. Both tap and bottled water come from rivers and _____ .

3. Bottled water is (**more** / **less**) expensive than tap water. It costs almost _____ times more.

4. Putting water in bottles (**saves** / **wastes**) a lot of water. Water is used to _____ the bottles.

5. (**18** / **80**) percent of plastic bottles go into the trash. This is very _____ for our planet.

Track 2-26
B. Listen for details. Listen and check your answers above.

Track 2-26
C. Listen for details. Reread the information in **A**. Complete the second sentences in **1–5** above with one word each. Then listen and check your answers.

D. Discuss with a partner. Is bottled water mostly good, mostly bad, or both good and bad? Why?

100

CONVERSATION

Track 2-27

A. Listen to the conversation.

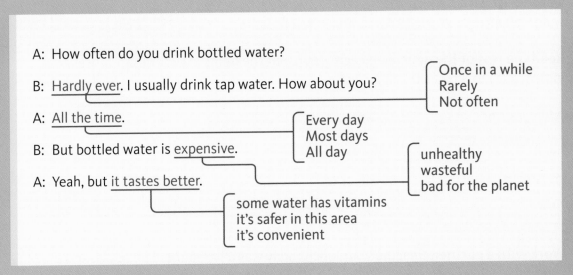

A: How often do you drink bottled water?

B: <u>Hardly ever</u>. I usually drink tap water. How about you?

> Once in a while
> Rarely
> Not often

A: <u>All the time</u>.

> Every day
> Most days
> All day

B: But bottled water is <u>expensive</u>.

> unhealthy
> wasteful
> bad for the planet

A: Yeah, but <u>it tastes better</u>.

> some water has vitamins
> it's safer in this area
> it's convenient

B. Practice with a partner. Use the words on the right.

C. Practice again with your partner. Talk about yourself.

Most plastic bottles finish up in the trash—or in the water, like in this lake in Romania.

Reading

A. Reading a chart. Look at the Water Costs chart on page 103. Which usually needs more water: plants (**green** boxes) or animals (**red** boxes)?

B. Read the rest of the article. In each group, put the items in order from **1** (uses the most water) to **3** (uses the least water).

A kilogram of:	One . . .
beef ____	apple ____
chocolate ____	cup of tea ____
rice ____	slice of bread ____

C. Work with a partner. Imagine your lunch today was a hamburger, an apple, and a cup of tea. How much water did you use? Does this information surprise you?

LISTENING

A. Listen for details. Read the three facts below. Guess the correct words in **blue**. Then listen and circle your answers.

Facts	knows	surprised
1. (**Brazil** / **Africa**) grows the most coffee in the world.	____	____
2. People first drank coffee in (**Arabia** / **Africa**).	____	____
3. To get one cup of coffee, you need (**47** / **147**) liters of water.	____	____

B. Listen for a speaker's attitude. Read sentences 1–3 in **A** again. Does the woman know each fact or is she surprised by it? Check **knows** or **is surprised by**.

C. Work with a partner. Whose food in a typical day uses more water, yours or your partner's?

DISCUSSION

Introducing surprising information. Work with a partner. **Turn to page 126.** **Student A**, tell your partner about your water facts. **Student B**, do the same. Use the language below.

> Did you know that you need 147 liters of water to get one cup of coffee?

> Are you serious? That's a lot.

We use a lot of water to make many different foods and drinks. For example, to make just one cup of tea, 30 liters (about 8 gallons) of water are needed! Farmers use most of that water for growing the tea plant. Here are some other examples:

To get a kilogram of chocolate, farmers use 24,000 liters of water.

To get a kilogram of beef, farmers use about 14,000 liters of water.

To get a kilogram of rice, farmers use 3,400 liters of water. Today, 21% of the world's water goes to growing rice.

Farmers use 1,279 liters of water to make just one hamburger.

To grow one apple, farmers need 70 liters of water.

To make one slice of bread, 40 liters of water are needed.

WATER COSTS
The amount of water needed to grow plants and raise animals.

VEGETABLES
MILK
FRUITS
PORK
EGGS
CHICKEN
SHEEP/GOAT
BEEF

Water on a coffee plant in Tanzania. To make one liter of coffee, farmers need 880 liters of water.

Amazing Water

People wash themselves in the Ganges River, in India.

About the video. This video answers some questions about water, including: *How much water is there on Earth? How much of this is fresh water (the kind we can drink)? How much water do we use to make and wash clothes? How is all the water on Earth connected?*

BEFORE YOU WATCH

Prediction. Read the sentences below and guess the correct answers.

1. Only (**3%** / **15%**) of Earth's water is fresh, and most of that is snow or ice.

2. So we have only (**1%** / **5%**) in rivers and lakes to use for drinking, washing, and other things.

3. You need (**270** / **2,700**) liters of water to make one cotton T-shirt. With that much water, a person can drink for (**90** / **900**) days.

4. You can use about (**150** / **1,500**) liters of water to wash your clothes.

While You Watch

A. Watch for details. Check your answers in **Before You Watch**.

B. What do you remember? Complete the information below using the words in the box.

clouds	cycle	ground	rain	sky	tap

1. Water (as _____ or snow) falls from the _____ in the sky.
2. The water goes into the _____, and in time, returns to the _____.
3. Because of this _____, water is always moving from place to place on Earth.
4. In time, water in the Ganges River in India can be the rain or _____ water in your city.

AFTER YOU WATCH

Work with a partner. Talk about a surprising fact from the video. Use your answers in **Before** and **After You Watch**. What information surprised you the most?

Did you know that only three percent of Earth's water is fresh?

I know. That's amazing.

all the water on Earth

fresh water in ice

water in lakes and rivers

There is very little fresh water on Earth in lakes and rivers to drink.

Your Personal Water Use

A public service announcement (PSA) is a TV, radio, or Internet advertisement with a message. You are going to make a PSA to tell people to save water.

A. Find out how much water you use. Work with a partner. **Turn to page 126** and ask your partner the questions in the questionnaire. Then get the total score for each section. Does your partner use a lot of water?

B. Make a short PSA. It can be a poster, video, or you can act it out.

1. Choose one area from the questionnaire. Think about ways people can save water in this area.

2. In your PSA, use facts you learned in this unit. Find other information online.

C. Show your PSA to the class. Which one is the best? Why?

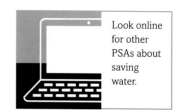

Look online for other PSAs about saving water.

> Did you know that meat uses a lot of water? To make one hamburger, we use 1,279 liters (338 gallons) of water. What can you do? Eat more vegetables!

Students use water bottles to make the word "steak." This is the water we need to make just one steak.

THINK ABOUT THE PHOTO

A. Complete the description. Look at the photo on the next page. Complete the information about the photo using the words in the box.

> first   goodbye   mats   parents   students   university

The people in this photo are the **1.** _____ of freshmen, or first-year
2. _____, at a(n) **3.** _____ in Wuhan, China. They do not
want to say **4.** _____ to their children and want to stay close to them on the
university campus on their **5.** _____ day of school. So the university puts out
about 300 **6.** _____ for families on the floor of the gymnasium.

B. Think of a title for this photo. Then share your title with the class and vote on the best one.

_____

DISCUSSION

A. Describe the photo. Work with a partner. Take turns describing the photo to each other.

> There are many mats.

> There are sleeping bags, too.

B. Discuss with a partner. What do you think of the parents in the photo? Would your parents do that? Would you like them to?

CAPTION COMPETITION

What do you think this
person is thinking?
Tell a partner.

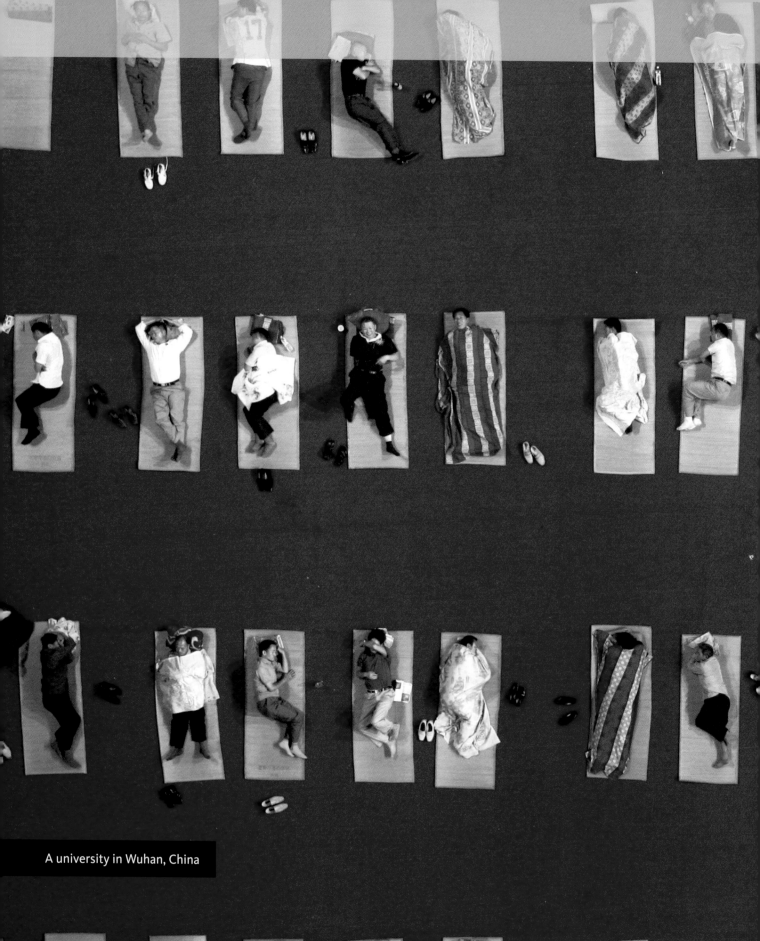

A university in Wuhan, China

Review 5

A. Complete the sentences. Use the words in the box. One word is extra.

> abroad   alone   college   independent   learned   math

1. I want to study _____. I think I'll study English in Australia this summer.

2. Kakenya Ntaiya went to _____ in the U.S.

3. _____ is my favorite subject, because I love numbers.

4. I prefer to work _____ on my project rather than with others.

5. I bought a car, because I _____ to drive last month.

B. Unscramble the letters to make words from Unit 10. Match the words to their definitions.

> telobdt   arhst   atp   tooleacch   tayehhl

1. The _____ is the place you put things that you no longer want or need.

2. Water from the faucet in the kitchen or bathroom is called _____ water.

3. I eat fresh vegetables every day. It is very _____.

4. _____ water is usually sold in a plastic container.

5. My favorite kind of icecream is _____. I love it!

C. Guess the school subject. Make a list of different school subjects. Then, have your partner guess which school subject you are talking about.

> In this subject, we study the past.

> Is it history?

> Yes, that's correct.

D. Work with a partner. Think of ways you can be more eco-friendly.

> We can save water by switching off the faucet when we brush our teeth.

> We can use bicycles instead of cars.

TARGET VOCABULARY

A **census** is an official count of the population of a country.
A group of people's **culture** is their beliefs, way of life, and arts.
If a group of things is **diverse**, it is made up of a wide variety of things.
One **foot** is 12 inches (about 30 centimeters).
An **immigrant** is a person who has come to live in a country from another country.
One **inch** is 2.54 centimeters.
If someone is **typical** of a group, they are the usual person of that group.
countries: Argentina, Brazil, China, Iran, Japan, Malaysia, the U.K., the U.S.
greetings: Hello.; Hi.; Hey.; It's nice to meet you.; It's great to meet you.
titles: Mr.; Miss; Ms.; Mrs.

IMPORTANT LANGUAGE

My name is Alex. **Your** name is Sofia. **His** name is Mr. Razak. **Her** name is Ms. Tanka.	**I** **You** **He** **She**	am are is is	a student	I am = **I'm** You are = **You're** He is = **He's** She is = **She's**
Our **Your** names are Alena **Their** and Liya.	**We** **You** **They**	are	students	We are = **We're** You are = **You're** They are = **They're**

Numbers							
0	zero	10	ten	20	twenty	30	thirty
1	one	11	eleven	21	twenty-one	40	forty
2	two	12	twelve	22	twenty-two	50	fifty
3	three	13	thirteen	23	twenty-three	60	sixty
4	four	14	fourteen	24	twenty-four	70	seventy
5	five	15	fifteen	25	twenty-five	80	eighty
6	six	16	sixteen	26	twenty-six	90	ninety
7	seven	17	seventeen	27	twenty-seven	100	one hundred
8	eight	18	eighteen	28	twenty-eight	1,000	one thousand
9	nine	19	nineteen	29	twenty-nine	1,000,000	one million

Asking for personal information

What's your name?
How do you spell that?
Where are you from?
How old are you?
Are you married or single?
What do you do?
How many people are there in your family?

PROJECT

Make a new survey. Choose a particular group of people in your country (e.g., business people, retired people, or young children). Make a survey and interview them. What is a typical person in that group like? Share your results with the class.

111

READING

Track 1-11

B. Split reading. Student B: Read about the Patagonian Expedition Race and complete the information about it in the table below.

Race	When and where is it?	What's good about it?	What's bad about it?
Rock and Roll Marathon	*in late* _____ _____		
Patagonian Expedition Race	*in* _____ _____		

Amazing Races

The Patagonian Expedition Race

Patagonia, South America

Good points. It's beautiful. Racers go through Patagonia. This place is famous for its amazing scenery. The race is also really exciting.

Bad points. It's *really* hard. Some say this is the world's most difficult race. It starts on February 14 and ends on the 22nd—eight days and 560 kilometers (350 miles) later.

People from around the world work in teams of four. They mountain bike, hike, and kayak for days. For many, it's very long and tiring. In fact, only half the teams finish this race each year.

C. Work with a partner. Ask your partner questions about the other race. Complete the chart. Then read about the other race to check your partner's answers.

A racer in the Patagonian Expeditio

TARGET VOCABULARY

A **costume** is a set of clothes you wear for a performance.

If a place is **crowded**, it is full of people.

An **event** is something that happens.

In a **marathon**, people race for 26 miles (about 42 kilometers).

If something is **popular**, a lot of people like it.

If you **prepare** for something, you get ready to do it.

A **prize** is something you get for winning a race.

A **race** is a competition to see who is the fastest.

A **trainer** teaches you to do something.

If you **win** a race, you finish first.

months: January, February, March, April, May, June, July, August, September, October, November, December

ordinal numbers: first, second, third, fourth, fifth, sixth, seventh, eighth, ninth, tenth, and so on

sports: basketball, bowling, golf, gymnastics, karate, hiking, running, skateboarding, skiing, soccer, surfing, swimming, taekwondo, tennis, yoga

IMPORTANT LANGUAGE

Making and replying to suggestions		
Let's watch tennis.	**Sounds good.**	**I don't know.** Tennis is kind of boring.

Talking about sports
play + **a sport** (usually one with a ball): play baseball, basketball, tennis, golf, soccer *I play soccer.*
do + **a type of exercise or martial art**: do gymnastics, do taekwondo, do yoga *She does gymnastics.*
go + **-ing word**: go bowling, skiing, swimming, etc. *We go skiing every February.*

Talking about likes and dislikes		
I **like** soccer. I **love** soccer.	**It's okay.**	I **don't like** soccer. I**'m not into** soccer. I **can't stand** soccer.

PROJECT

Make a poster. Make a poster for the sports event you talked about in the extension activity. Use photos from the Internet. Show your poster to your friends to get their comments. Then, when you are finished, show the final poster to your class.

DISCUSSION

Talking about how often you do things. Ask your partner about his or her sleep habits.

	always	usually	sometimes	never
1. Do you sleep 8 to 9 hours at night?				
2. Do you need a strong cup of coffee or tea to wake up in the morning?				
3. Do you watch TV or movies in bed?				
4. Do you stay awake late playing video games, surfing the Web, or chatting online?				

TARGET VOCABULARY

A **cinema** or **movie theater** is a place where you can see a movie.

An **early bird** is a person who likes waking up early.

An **energetic** person has a lot of energy.

Karaoke is an activity where people sing a popular song in front of their friends.

A **night market** is a place, often outdoors, where you can buy things in the evening.

A **night owl** is a person who likes staying awake late at night.

A **nightclub** is a place where people go late in the evening to dance.

Your **routine** is the usual list of things you do each day at particular times.

A **teenager** is a person aged from 13 to 19.

adverbs of frequency: never, sometimes, often, usually, always

days of the week: Monday, Tuesday, Wednesday, Thursday, Friday, Saturday, Sunday

IMPORTANT LANGUAGE

Talking about time			
What time is it? **It's . . .**			
4:00	four (o'clock)	**4:30**	four thirty
4:05	four oh five / five after four	**4:35**	four thirty-five
4:10	four ten / ten after four	**4:40**	four forty / twenty to five
4:15	four fifteen / quarter after four	**4:45**	four forty-five / quarter to five
4:20	four twenty	**4:50**	four fifty / ten to five
4:25	four twenty-five	**4:55**	four fifty-five / five to five

The park opens **at** 10:00 a.m. and closes **at** midnight.
The park is open **on** Saturday / **on** the weekend.
It's open **in** the morning / afternoon / evening.
        at night.
The store is open **from** 9:00 to 11:00 p.m.
The store is open **until** 11:00 p.m.
The restaurant is open **all day** / **twenty-four hours** / **day and night**.
Let's go to a movie **today** / **tonight** / **tomorrow**.
The store closes **early**—at 3:00 p.m.
It closes **late**—at midnight.
Class starts at 9:00 and it's 8:30. We're **early**.
Class starts at 9:00 and it's 9:30. We're **late**!

PROJECT

Interview a night shift worker. Find people who work (or used to work) the night shift. Interview them to find out what a typical day is like for them. Make a presentation about the people. Include photos. Show your presentation to the class and ask them which night job they think is best and which job they think is worst.

TARGET VOCABULARY

Casual clothes are ones you usually wear at home or vacation, and not for formal events.

A **designer** is a person who designs things, usually by making drawings of them.

If something is **dirty**, it is not clean.

A **fashion** or **style** is a way of dressing.

Fashionable or **stylish** clothes are modern and nice-looking.

If something is **in fashion**, it is popular now.

A **scientist** is someone who studies science.

If you **wash** something, you clean it using water.

kinds of clothes: boots, cap, coat, handbag, hat, jacket, jeans, pants, scarf, shirt, shoes, skirt, stockings, suit, sunglasses

IMPORTANT LANGUAGE

Talking about clothes	
What is he/she wearing?	**He's wearing** blue jeans **and** a white T-shirt.
	She's wearing a T-shirt **with** the name of a band.
When do you wear special clothes?	**We wear** special clothes on holidays.

Describing clothing and fashion	
It's . . . / It looks . . .	
They're . . . / They look . . .	
positive meaning	**negative meaning**
casual	cheap / tacky
comfortable	ugly
cool	uncomfortable
stylish	weird

PROJECT

Keep a research diary. Observe the people around you—people in coffee shops, people on the train, people in shops. Look at what they are wearing. Keep a diary. What clothing and clothing accessories are the most common? Share your findings with the class.

READING

Track 1-27

B. Split reading. Student B: Read "Tiny Houses." Answer questions **1–4** in the chart below about tiny houses.

	container housing	the tiny house
1. How big is it?		
2. How many rooms are there?		
3. Is it expensive?		
4. In your opinion, how many people can live in it?		

Today, 50% of the people on Earth live in cities. By 2030, it will be 60%. With more people in cities, there is less space, and housing costs more. What can we do? Here's an idea.

TINY HOUSES

In the U.S., Jay Shafer makes tiny houses for people. The smallest is only 9 square meters (98 square feet). The houses are small, but they have everything you need. On the first floor, there is a kitchen, a living area, and a bathroom. On the second floor is a bedroom. It is big enough for two people. The houses are also inexpensive. Most are $15,000.

C. Work in pairs. Ask your partner questions to complete the rest of the chart.

117

TARGET VOCABULARY

If something is **green** or **eco-friendly**, it is kind to the environment.
If a house is **furnished**, it has furniture.
If you **save energy**, you are careful not to use too much electricity.
If you **waste energy**, you use more electricity than you need.
actions for electricity: turn on, turn off, plug in, unplug
appliances: air conditioner (A/C), blender, coffee maker, dishwasher, dryer, heater, iron, kettle, lamp, oven, refrigerator, washing machine
electronics: computer, phone, phone charger, printer, stereo, TV, video game machine
furniture: blinds, cabinet, chair, curtains, rug, sofa, table
housing locations: downtown, neighborhood, suburbs
kinds of housing: apartment, dormitory (dorm), high-rise, house, studio apartment
parts of a room: ceiling, door, floor, wall, window
rooms in a house: balcony, bathroom, kitchen, living room, master bedroom, second bedroom

IMPORTANT LANGUAGE

Prepositions of place: *in, on, near*
The Kim family lives **in** an apartment building. It's **in** Gangnam, a neighborhood **in** Seoul. The Martinez family lives **in** a house **in** the suburbs. The Kims' apartment is **on** the 12th floor. The Martinez family lives **on** San Pedro Road. His apartment is **near** school. The living room is **near** the kitchen.

PROJECT

Design a home for your friend. Interview your friend or classmate about his or her dream home (e.g. *Where is it? How many rooms are there?*). Draw the floor plan. Explain your plan to the class.

TARGET VOCABULARY

If you **bargain** with someone, you talk to them and try to get a low price.

A **coupon** is a piece of paper that you use to pay less for something.

Something **local** to an area is from that area.

A **product** is something that people make and sell.

Psychology is the science of studying people's minds.

A **sample** of something is a small amount of it that shows you what it is like.

A **souk** is a marketplace in the Middle East.

A **souvenir** is something you buy and bring home from a trip.

A **time limit** is the time in which you are allowed to do something.

Tourists are people who visit another place on vacation.

units of currency: yen, dollar, pound, dirham

IMPORTANT LANGUAGE

Asking for and giving prices

How much is this?
It's $200.
They're $200.
That's too expensive. Do you have anything **cheaper**?

Pointing to something

Is **this** your wallet?
Can I see **that** shirt?
How much are **these** shoes?
Can you please show me **those** earrings?

Do you ever?

Do you ever buy things online?
Yeah, sometimes.
No, never.

PROJECT

Make a TV ad. Record a video to make an ad for the shop you prepared in the **Expansion Activity** on page 66. Use photos and/or music in your ad. Show the video to a friend to get feedback. Then make any changes and put the ad on an online video hosting site or show it to the class.

READING

Track 2-10

B. Split reading. Student B: Read the passage below.

Cold Weather Blues

Some people feel unhappy in bad weather.

It's 11:00 a.m. on a cold, rainy day and you're at home. You decide to clean your room and do homework. By 3:00 p.m., the weather is still bad, but your work is done. This isn't surprising. On bad-weather days, some people are more energetic, say scientists. In the cold weather, they feel more awake, so they work more and think better.

But for others, bad weather is a problem. Some people feel sleepy or sad. Scientists think that this happens because of a chemical in our body called serotonin. In the bright sunlight, serotonin increases in our body and we feel awake. But in less sunlight (for example, on a cloudy or rainy day), serotonin decreases. Then some people feel tired. Others feel blue. For these people, winter can be a difficult time.

C. Reading comprehension. Student B: Answer questions **3** and **4** below. Ask your partner questions to answer questions **1** and **2**.

1. On a sunny day, most people feel (**happy / lazy**), because warm, sunny weather (**relaxes us / makes us less energetic**).

2. On a hot day, we think more (**quickly / slowly**), so it is (**easier / harder**) to think clearly.

3. On rainy days, some people are (**more / less**) energetic, so they (**are able to work better / feel more lazy**).

4. On cloudy or rainy days, the amount of the chemical serotonin in our body (**increases / decreases**). This can make us feel (**tired or blue / happier and more energetic**).

DISCUSSION

Conversation Ideas

1. It's a hot, sunny day. You want to go out, but you have to study for a test. You feel cranky and can't think clearly.

2. The weather is terrible and you feel blue. Today is another cold, rainy day. You want to go to the gym and exercise, but you're feeling tired and lazy.

TARGET VOCABULARY

If you feel **blue**, you feel sad.
A **calm** person doesn't show or feel any worry or anger.
A **cranky** person feels angry very easily.
When something **decreases**, it becomes smaller.
When something **increases,** it becomes bigger.
If someone is **lazy**, they do not want to do any work.
When you **relax**, you feel less worried.
seasons: spring, summer, fall (autumn), winter, rainy season, dry season

IMPORTANT LANGUAGE

Talk about the weather				
	Noun	**Adjective**	**Verb**	
	a cloud	cloudy	—	**It's cloudy / sunny** today.
	rain	rainy	rain	**It's raining / snowing** today.
	snow	snowy	snow	**It rains / snows** a lot in the winter.
	sun	sunny	—	The **sun is shining** today.
	wind	windy	—	The **wind is blowing** really hard this morning. **It's** usually **windy** in the spring.

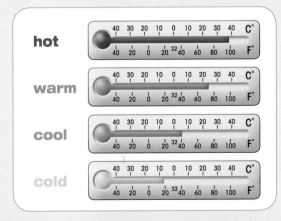

hot

warm

cool

cold

PROJECT

Make a brochure. Choose a different city. Find out information about the weather and what visitors can do in different seasons in the city. Make a brochure to tell people about the city and to make them want to visit. Show your brochure to your class. Do they want to visit this city?

B. Finish the passage. Check your idea in **A.**
Track 2-17

The **Wow!** Signal
Did aliens try to contact us?

At 10:16 p.m., Big Ear got a very powerful signal from space. How powerful? Think of it this way: imagine listening to soft music on the radio, and then suddenly it becomes very loud. The signal was unusual because it was very "loud." Also, it lasted for almost a minute and a half. Ehman was very surprised. On the report, he wrote the word *"Wow!"*

The signal came from outside our solar system, say scientists. Where exactly? We don't know. Was it a message from another planet? Maybe, but even now, scientists are not sure. We only got the signal one time. Scientists continue to study the skies, but for now, the Wow! signal is still a mystery.

C. Reading comprehension. Complete the questions below, using the past tense. Then work with a partner. Take turns asking and answering them.

1. Who (**Jerry Ehman / be**) _____*was Jerry Ehman*_____?

2. Where (**he / work**) _____?

3. What (**be / Big Ear**) _____?

4. What (**happen**) _____ on August 15 at 10:16 p.m.?

5. How long (**the signal / last**) _____?

6. Where (**the signal / come**) _____ from?

7. How many times (**we / get**) _____ the signal?

D. Work with a partner. Read the question under the title of the passage again. What is your answer? Why?

TARGET VOCABULARY

If something is **ancient**, it is very old.

A **bomb** is something that explodes and destroys a large area.

If someone **contacts** you, they call you on the phone or send you a message.

An **experience** is something that you do or that happens to you.

An **explosion** is a sudden burst of energy that damages things.

Something that is **giant** is very big.

The **government** of a country is the group of people who control it.

Proof is something that shows that something is true or exists.

If you **recreate** something, you make it exist again.

Something that is **scary** is frightening.

A **signal** is a sign that gives a message to the person who gets it.

IMPORTANT LANGUAGE

Past tense			
	Present	**Past**	**Past negative**
with *be*	is	was	wasn't
	are	were	weren't
regular verbs	believe	believed	*didn't* + base form of the present verb:
	listen	listened	• didn't believe
	live	lived	• didn't live
	look	looked	• didn't walk
	move	moved	
	walk	walked	

IMPORTANT LANGUAGE

Past tense (continued)			
Present	**Past**		**Past negative**
irregular verbs	come	came	*didn't* + base form of the present verb:
	get	got	• didn't come
	have/has	had	• didn't see
	hear	heard	• didn't write
	make	made	
	say	said	
	see	saw	
	think	thought	
	write	wrote	

Express certainty
Do you think the Yeti is real?

Definitely.	Yes, I think it is true or real.
Probably.	
Maybe.	
I doubt it.	No, I don't think it is true or real.

Tell a story	
Start your story	**Continue your story**
Yesterday . . .	At first . . .
A week/month/year ago . . .	After that . . .
In 2013 . . .	(And, so, but) then . . .
Last week/month/year/summer . . .	Suddenly . . .
One day/night . . .	Later . . .

PROJECT

Collect more theories. Interview different people about the mystery you talked about on page 86. Find out their theories. Decide which are the most believable or unbelievable theories and share them with the class. Do other students find the theories believable?

TARGET VOCABULARY

A **generation** is all the people in a group or country who are of a similar age.

When you **grow up**, you become older.

If someone is **independent**, they do not need help from anyone else.

If someone does an **internship** at a company, they work there while they are studying, as part of their course.

Your **major** is your main subject of study in college. You major in a subject.

A **tutor** is someone who teaches one student or a small group of students.

college majors: business, education, engineering, English, law, science

kinds of school: art school, cooking (culinary) school, cram school, driving school, language institute, music academy, law school, medical school

school grades: kindergarten, elementary school, middle school (junior high), high school, college/university

school subjects: math, science, history, English, P.E.

IMPORTANT LANGUAGE

Talking about education
I **learned** to speak Spanish in college. Now I'm **taking a class** in a language institute.
We **learned** about Mayan art in high school.
Mr. Kim **teaches** kindergarten.
He **teaches** children to read.

Talking about ability
Can you / **Do you know how to** drive?
Yes, I can. / **Yes, I know how** (to drive).
No, not really. / **No, not very well**.
No, I can't. / **No, I never learned how** (to drive).

PROJECT

Make a video. Find out what amazing abilities your friends and family have. Ask them if it is okay to record them. Make a video to introduce each person and his or her amazing talent. Share your video with your classmates.

DISCUSSION

Introduce and reply to surprising information.

> Did you know (that) a billion people don't have clean drinking water?

> Yeah, I know. > Really? > Are you serious/kidding? > That's amazing. > No way!

WATER FACTS

Student A

1. You need a lot of water to make paper. For example, you need 1,249 liters of water to make a 125-page book.

2. We're drinking the same water as the dinosaurs. Three hundred million years ago, Earth had the same water.

Student B

1. Each time you flush the toilet, you use 9.5 liters of water.

2. The Earth is 70% water. But only 3% is fresh water.

EXPANSION ACTIVITY

WATER USE QUESTIONNAIRE

HOME: How often do you . . .			
1. take a shower?	a. 5 times a week	b. every day	c. more than once a day
2. wash your hair?	a. once a week	b. twice a week	c. every day
3. brush your teeth with the water on?	a. never	b. once in a while	c. all the time
			Total score: _____

DIET: How often do you . . .			
1. eat meat each week?	a. never	b. once or twice	c. three times or more
2. drink bottled water?	a. never	b. once in a while	c. all the time
3. drink coffee or tea in a day?	a. never	b. once or twice	c. three times or more
			Total score: _____

SHOPPING: How often do you buy. . .			
1. new clothes each year?	a. once or less	b. twice	c. three times or more
2. paper products each month?	a. once or less	b. twice	c. three times or more
3. electronics each year?	a. once or less	b. twice	c. three times or more
			Total score: _____

Answers: **a** = 1 point   **b** = 2 points   **c** = 3 points

• **3–4 points total:** Good for you! You don't use a lot of water.
• **5–6 points total:** Your water use is average.   • **7–9 points total:** You use too much water.

TARGET VOCABULARY

One **gallon** is about 3.8 liters.

Paper products are things like books, notebooks, and printer paper.

Plastic is a light but strong material made from chemicals.

Trash is all the things you don't want or need, for example, old food or waste paper.

We use water to . . . brush our teeth, take a shower or bath, flush the toilet, do laundry (wash clothes), make coffee, tea, and other drinks, raise animals (for food), cook, wash dishes, have fun (go swimming)

IMPORTANT LANGUAGE

How often . . . ? / frequency expressions

How often do you drink bottled water?

(I drink bottled water) **all the time.** = **always**
                                once in a while. = **sometimes**

I **never/hardly ever** drink bottled water.

How often do you do laundry?
(I do laundry) every day / week / Saturday / weekend.
                once / twice / three, four, five times a week/month/year.

Countable and uncountable nouns

Countable nouns	apple/apples; cup/cups
Uncountable nouns	rice, water, milk, tea, coffee
Counting uncountable nouns	**A glass of** water, milk, wine **A cup of** coffee, tea **A can of** soda **A piece of** chicken, cheese, chocolate, paper **A slice of** bread **A kilogram of** rice, beef, chicken

Introduce and reply to surprising information

Did you know (that) it takes 70 liters of water to grow one apple?

Yeah, I know.

Really? / Are you serious/kidding? /
That's incredible. / No way! / That's amazing.

PROJECT

Keep a personal "water diary."
Keep a record of your water usage for a week and try and save water. Find out more ways you can save water. Interview family and friends, or look for information online. Share your diary with your class.

Credits

Photo Credits

1 Stephen Alvarez/NGC, **3**, **103** Roy Toft/NGC, **4-5**, **80** (bg) Gordon Wiltsie/NGC, **11** Prof. Stan Z. Li and his research team of the Center for Biometrics and Security Research, **12** (clockwise, from top) Vladan Milisavljevic/Getty Images, John and Tina Reid/Getty Images, Afrog Design Unit/Getty Images, Chris Maclean/Getty Images, Stephen Alvarez/NGC, **14** (clockwise, from top left) Frans Lanting/NGC, Nicolas McComber/Getty Images, OtnaYdur/Shutterstock.com, Aaron Huey/NGC, **15** Juan Camilo Bernal/Shutterstock.com, **16** Spencer Platt/Getty Images, **17** (t) National Geographic Society, (b) Mario Tama/Getty Images, **18** Michael S. Lewis/NGC, **19** Kai Pfaffenbach/Reuters, **20** Christinne Muschi GMH/HB/Reuters, **21** Christophe Ena/AP Photo, **22** Ethan Miller/Getty Images, **23** (l to r) Aspen Photo/Shutterstock.com, Natursports/Shutterstock.com, **23** Neale Cousland/Shutterstock.com, **24** David Edwards/NGC, **25** Nicolas Reynard/NGC, **26** Filippo Monteforte/AFP/Getty Images, **27**, **28-29** Toru Hanai/Reuters, **31** Paul Chesley/NGC, **32** (t) Kelly Cheng Travel Photography/Getty Images, (b) Saad Shalash/Reuters, **33** Stephen Alvarez/NGC, **34** Joel Sartore/NGC, **35** Alen Ajan/Flickr/Getty Images, **36** Circlephoto/Shutterstock.com, **37** Maggie Steber/NGC, **38** Gonzalo Arroyo/Getty Images, **39** Philippe Wojazer/Reuters, **40** (clockwise, from top left) Catherine Karnow/NGC, Justin Guariglia/NGC, David Alan Harvey/NGC, **42** (clockwise, from top left) Cornell University/AP Photo, Rex Features via AP Images, Joel Sartore/NGC, **43** (l to r) Blend Images/Shutterstock.com, Fabrizio Bensch/Reuters, Kimihiro Hoshino/AFP/Getty Images, **44** Tino Soriano/NGC, **45** (l to r) John Scofield/NGC, Lori Epstein/NGC, Marcel Jancovic/Shutterstock.com, **46** Joel Ryan/Invision/AP Images, **47**, **48-49** Chris McGrath/Getty Images, **51** Jim Richardson/NGC, **52-53** Yeondoo Jung, **55** (t) Horizons WWP/Alamy, (b) Pics-xl/Shutterstock.com, **56** atm2003/Shutterstock.com, **57** udra11/Shutterstock.com, **58** Diane Cook and Len Jenshel/NGC, **59** Justin Guariglia/NGC, **60** (clockwise, from top) Yadid Levy/Getty Images, Martin Kreuzer/Getty Images, Nico Traut/Shutterstock.com, **62** (t to b) Larry Downing/Reuters, Suzanne Plunkett/Reuters, Jacobs Stock Photography/Getty Images, **63** (l to r) Barone Firenze/Shutterstock.com, jmarkow/Shutterstock.com, hotzone/Shutterstock.com, **64** Symphonie/The Image Bank/Getty Images, **65** Chantal de Bruijne/Shutterstock.com, **66** Radu Bercan/Shutterstock.com, **67**, **68-69** Thierry Roge/Reuters, **71** Cotton Coulson - Keen Press/NGC, **72** Michael Melford/NGC, **73** Matthew Micah Wright/Getty Images, **74** Paul Hackett/Reuters, **76** (t) Mohsin Raza/Reuters, **77** Marko Djurica/Reuters, **78** David Min/Shutterstock.com, **79** Keystone/Hutton Archive/Getty Images, **80** (inset) Topical Press Agency/Getty Images, **81** (both) Joel Sartore/NGC, **82**, **122** John A Davis/Shutterstock.com, **83** (l) Toshifumi Kitamura/AFP/Getty Images, (r) STR New/Reuters, **86** Ho New/Reuters, **87**, **88-89** Raul Touzon/NGC, **91** Maggie Steber/NGC, **92** ranplett/Vetta/Getty Images, **93** (t) Mark Theissen/NGC, (b) Andrew Castellano/Flickr Vision/Getty Images, **94** Design Pics Inc/NGC, **95** Cary Wolinsky/NGC, **96** Mattias Klum/NGC, **97** Mujahid Safodien/Reuters, **98** Nando Machado/Shutterstock.com, **99** Robb Kendrick/NGC, **100** David Mdzinarishvili/Reuters, **101** Stephane Bidouze/Shutterstock.com, **104** Aleksandar Todorovic/Shutterstock.com, **105** Anton Balazh/Shutterstock.com, **106** Charles Platiau/Reuters, **107**, **108-109** Stringer/China Out/Reuters, **112** Will Gray/Reuters, **117** Zuma Press, Inc./Alamy, **120** Steve Raymer/NGC, **121** sahua d/Shutterstock.com

NGC = National Geographic Creative

Illustration Credits

13, **16**, **22**, **24**, **44**, **56**, **60**, **64**, **72**, **76**, **78**, **84**, **92**, **96**, **112** National Geographic Maps, **13** (flags) Ints Vikmanis/Shutterstock.com, **53**, **103**, **121** Page2 LLC, **76** (b) Nikitina Olga/Shutterstock.com, **84** kbeis/Vetta/Getty Images, **85** Mark Garlick/Getty Images

Text Credits

13 Adapted from "7 Billion: Are You Typical" by National Geographic (http://video.nationalgeographic.com/video/specials/sitewide-redesign/ngm-7billion/); **22** Adapted from "Rock & Roll Marathon in Las Vegas" (http://adventure.nationalgeographic.com/adventure/trips/best-adventure-races-2012/); **34** Adapted from "Early Birds, Night Owls: Blame Your Genes." National Geographic News. January 28, 2008. (http://news.nationalgeographic.com/news/2008/01/080126-sleep-genes.html); **42** Adapted from "Smart Shirts," by Stuart Thornton (http://education.nationalgeographic.com/education/news/smart-shirts/?ar_a=1) and "Mosquito Proof Clothing to Combat Malaria" (http://earthweek.com/2012/ew120525/ew120525g.html); **55** Adapted from "Amsterdam's Lean, Green Shipping Container Homes." (http://environment.nationalgeographic.com/environment/sustainable-earth/pictures-amsterdam-shipping-container-homes); **74** Adapted from "Why Summer Makes Us Lazy" (http://www.newyorker.com/online/blogs/elements/2013/07/psychology-why-summer-makes-us-lazy.html) and "Global Warming Making People More Aggressive?" (http://news.nationalgeographic.com/news/2010/03/100324-global-warming-violence-aggression/); **82**, **122** Adapted from "What Is the Wow! Signal?" (http://channel.nationalgeographic.com/channel/chasing-ufos/articles/what-is-the-wow-signal/); **93** Adapted from "Kakenya Ntaiya, Educator" (http://www.nationalgeographic.com/explorers/bios/kakenya-ntaiya/); **94** Adapted from "Photo Camp" (http://photography.nationalgeographic.com/photography/photocamp); **102** Adapted from How Much H_2O Is Embedded in Everyday Life" (http://environment.nationalgeographic.com/environment/freshwater/embedded-water/); **112** Adapted from "Patagonian Expedition Race" (http://adventure.nationalgeographic.com/adventure/trips/best-adventure-races-2012/); **117** Adapted from "Tiny House, Happy Life" (http://newswatch.nationalgeographic.com/2012/12/10/tiny-house-happy-life/); **120** Adapted from "Blue Light Special" (http://phenomena.nationalgeographic.com/2010/10/26/blue-light-special/)